2013

The Teach Yourself series has been trusted around the world
for over 60 years. This new series of 'In a Week' business books
is designed to help people at all levels and around the world to

f   rn in

a

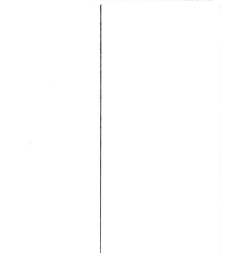

Peter Maskrey and Geoff Ribbens share a professional background in Human Resource Management (HRM) in both the private and public sectors. They have known each other since the early 1970s and have frequently worked together, training clients in various skills including how to find and then secure a job. In this book they aim to share their vast wealth of knowledge and experience with a wider audience, and hope it will be of use to both those who are recruiting as well as the individual seeking a new job or career.

Finding your next job

Peter Maskrey and
Geoff Ribbens

www.inaweek.co.uk

Teach Yourself®

Typeset by Cenveo Publisher Services.

Printed in Great Britain by CPI Group (UK) Ltd, Croydon, CR0 4YY.

Hodder & Stoughton policy is to use papers that are natural, renewable and recyclable products and made from wood grown in sustainable forests. The logging and manufacturing processes are expected to conform to the environmental regulations of the country of origin.

Hodder & Stoughton Ltd

338 Euston Road

London NW1 3BH

www.hodder.co.uk

Contents

Introduction

The main reason for writing this book has been to help people looking for a new job to get organized, think about why they want to work, what they want to do, what they can do (realistically) and then marshal all of that information into getting a job.

We start the book on 'Sunday', with a discussion about how you feel and discuss emotions, because if you are looking for a new job you might feel dissatisfied with your present role or you may have been made redundant. It is important to recognize these feelings and not let negative emotions get in the way of constructive actions. We also provide a checklist of financial issues.

'Monday' explores the CV (or resumé). Some employers feel that who you have worked for in the past is more important than your unique skills and abilities, whilst other employers are more interested in your skills and abilities. We suggest that the CV should be succinct; it is a sales document to get you the interview not a life history.

On 'Tuesday' we ask you to examine your individual strengths and weaknesses. This helps you decide on your new job or career and provides some of the things you might include in the CV mostly emphasizing your strengths. It also looks at the opportunities and threats to you as a person seeking a new job.

'Wednesday' considers job search techniques from looking at business directories to using your social networks, which can be very fruitful for many people. We also mention use of the internet as well as other imaginative routes.

'Thursday' we explore applying for jobs, application forms and prospecting letters. We also look at the issue of maintaining motivation in the job search.

On 'Friday' we point out that employers seek motivated people. There are six key areas at work which are motivational and you need to understand these six areas to come across as motivated. We then consider the complexity of the interview itself and how to respond to questions.

Finally on 'Saturday' we discuss issues to do with those who contemplate self employment, which may be a temporary solution or permanent.

SUNDAY

Moving on

In essence there are two main reasons why you might want to seek a new job: you are dissatisfied with your present job or, for whatever reason, you find yourself unemployed. In both cases you need to understand your feelings and emotions – changing jobs, being forced to change jobs or even seeking your first job has a psychological impact.

In most cases there is a rollercoaster of emotions ranging from elation to fear, to depression and even stress and anger. For those of us who have experienced unemployment, it is a difficult but worthwhile thinking process to try to see it more as an opportunity than a threat. Your situation is actually giving you a chance to review what you really want to do when it comes to your next job (or your first); to think about your motivation and be aware of your expectations. Try to be optimistic but also realistic.

Why move on?

There are many reasons why people move on from one job to the next. Some are honourable, some are unavoidable and some are a matter of expediency – that is, you jump before you are pushed!

Some individuals move because they have achieved as much as they can and are seeking more of a challenge; their present job is no longer motivating and there are few or no chances for promotion. Other individuals may see no future with their present employer as it may be downsizing and the market for the company's products and services is diminishing.

People sometimes just feel they need to move on for different work experiences and may think that a change will make them more marketable. Some people may be generally dissatisfied and want to move out of their present situation and start afresh. Finally, there are those who have no choice, because their job has become redundant or they have been dismissed for some other reason.

Those people leaving a job voluntarily generally do so because they have something else to go on to. For those whose job has become redundant, there is no choice and we will look at this first.

Feelings and emotions after redundancy

For the majority of people, being made redundant generates a multitude of feelings such as frustration, relief, excitement, hostility, aggression, stress, disappointment, self-criticism and depression. Mixed with these negative feelings there are occasionally some positive ones such as anticipation and a firm vision for a new working life. The normal response to being made redundant is often a combination of mood swings which can make life difficult. Another annoying aspect of being made redundant is that friends and relatives are often full of 'good ideas' about what you should do. Some individuals will suggest you have been badly treated and that 'you should fight it' or 'take your employer to a tribunal'. Or there is the optimist who will suggest that 'it's a great opportunity' and that you should seek a job in tune with your hobbies and interests: 'You have always liked bird watching, why don't you get a job bird watching?' In some cases a normally patient and placid individual, when hearing such suggestions, will turn on the 'well meaning' adviser and tell them what type of job they ought to go for – especially if it involves running, jumping and a nearby lake!

Emotional responses to losing a job are on a broad spectrum – it's important to recognize your response as normal – and move on

Frustration

The most common response to redundancy is a feeling of frustration, as you are prevented from achieving the things you desire. Frustration results from a blocked goal and there are three normal responses.

1 **Problem-solving behaviour.** 'I will seek a new job.' This is a positive response and sometimes has some very useful outcomes. A typical problem-solving approach may be to still work for your employer but on a freelance basis. Another approach might be to use the redundancy money to set up your own business or change your career.

2 **Aggression directed at others.** We all have a psychological contract with our employer. We will be hard working and loyal as long as we are treated fairly and paid the rate for the job! When an employer makes us redundant it is like

a rejection. The company has broken the psychological contract with us, similar to a divorce. The trouble with the psychological contract is that it is not in writing and we feel betrayed. How often have you heard people say, 'I have worked for that company for 20 years and I have been cast out like a piece of rubbish through no fault of my own'? In some cases employees do not direct their aggression at the abstract organization they have just left, but they become aggressive and impatient with those around them, maybe even their friends and family!

3 **Aggression directed at oneself.** Some individuals direct their aggression inwardly, blaming themselves for their situation and becoming depressed. In extreme cases suicidal feelings can result from being made redundant, as people cannot cope with the doubt and uncertainty about the future. They feel that they have let their families down and it was somehow their fault.

For most of us, the feelings and emotions we experience might well be a combination of all those above as we move in and out of pessimism and optimism. To remain sane, we have to accept that the feelings described above are normal and to be expected. We could, of course, try to direct our energies onto the problem-solving approach as this is much more likely to generate positive outcomes.

Relief

In some cases people experience a sense of relief. This may arise because the job had become a mental burden and suddenly the load has been lifted. The individual is relieved that the decision to leave has been made for them. They may not have wanted to take the risk of resigning or were too busy to seek a new position but now their employer has made the decision for them.

Excitement

This might seem odd but some people, especially if they have had a substantial payoff, have a feeling of excitement and adventure. In this case they look at life afresh and see positive opportunities for the future. This excitement can also be mixed with stress and depression – a roller coaster ride of the emotions!

Stress

Another normal response to being made redundant is to feel stressed. The trouble with stress is that it tends to creep up on us and often other people notice the symptoms before we do. Stress occurs when a person's natural resources cannot cope with the demands made upon them.

Holmes and Rahe (T. H. Holmes and R.H. Rahe [1967], 'Stress Rating Scale', *Journal of Psychosomatic Research*, 11 pp 213–18) carried out research into the causes of stress. They sampled 5000 people and found the following life events caused the most stress. Each life event was given a value with the most stressful event being given a value of 100. The life events were identified as follows:

Death of spouse	100
Divorce	73
Marital separation	65
Death of family member	63
Personal injury or illness	53
Fired at work	47

The symptoms of stress can be as follows: **irritability, resentment, feelings of panic, anxiety, guilt, depression, lack of concentration** and **difficulty in making decisions**. In addition to these mental symptoms, there are also physical symptoms such as **high blood pressure, lack of appetite, indigestion, inability to sleep, headaches** and **excessive tiredness**.

> *'Out of the gloom a voice said unto me, "Smile and be happy, things could be worse." So I smiled and was happy and, behold, things did get worse!'*

What can we do about our feelings?

The way to cope with the inevitable feelings described previously is to do the following:

1 Recognize that *these feelings are normal* and totally understandable.
2 Do not allow your energies to be directed into aggression towards others or yourself, but *use that drive and energy for problem solving* – finding a job.
3 If you are excessively tired, recognize it as a symptom of stress and not an illness. *Take some rest breaks* during the day so you can be refreshed for the next task.
4 *Take some physical exercise* to get rid of that excess energy and keep physically fit. Sitting around all day will exaggerate negative thoughts and feelings.

Redundancy – why me?

The word 'redundancy' refers to the fact that the job you are doing is no longer required. It is important, therefore, to realize that *it is the job that is no longer required* not *you* personally. Rapid commercial, industrial and technological changes in recent years have made redundancy very common and it has much less of a stigma attached now than it had twenty years ago.

There are, occasionally, other reasons why your job, in particular, has become redundant. It is important that you face up to some of the other possible reasons before you make the same mistake again.

1 It could be that you have been selected for redundancy because you were in the wrong job in the first place. In comparison with others, you may not have performed so well. The authors of this book carry out redundancy counselling and we regularly encounter individuals who are actually thankful that their jobs became redundant because it forced them to look for jobs in which they would be happier and more motivated.

Always remember, it's jobs that are made redundant, not people

2 Your job may have been selected for redundancy because senior management did not value your contribution. In their eyes you did not add value. Similarly, it may be that you are able to manage your own team but you do not have the skills of 'managing up'. That is, managing the boss. You may be the type of person who is politically naïve. You may not have pushed yourself forward as others have.

3 Another reason for being selected for redundancy is that, compared with other people, you have been perceived as 'difficult'. In this case, you might be very good, full of bright ideas but at the same time 'challenging' to your boss and to your colleagues. Some organizations value such innovative people, whilst others dislike those who 'rock the boat' or challenge the status quo. We often find people who have been made 'redundant' because they are, in effect, 'too good' and the boss feels threatened.

Apart from clear cases of unfair dismissal, it is probably better to leave your organization in good heart and, above all, with good references. Think ahead to a better working life and try to leave behind any feelings of injustice and resentment.

Financial issues

Following redundancy, you are likely to receive some form of financial compensation from your employer if you reside in the UK and you should aim to find an alternative job as quickly as you can to benefit from your financial termination package. In order to do so you must assume that it may take some time to find a new job. So use the money wisely. You must also budget to retain as much of the redundancy pay as you can and continue to survive financially in the interim. You may be out of work for four to six months and perhaps longer.

Look at the Budget Plan below. Under the heading **Current income (all sources)**, enter the amount of salary after tax you have received in redundancy pay, outstanding holiday entitlement pay and any other money you have received in your final month against box 1. If you receive interest on any investments, dividends, savings or any other regular amounts of money (after tax), enter that against item 2. Do the same in item 3 for any other amounts of money (like building society, bank or other savings accounts) from any sources other than those already entered against items 1 and 2. Add all those up and enter the total amount in the **Total receipts** box.

Next, record all your monthly expenditure under the **Current regular expenditure** heading for each of the numbered items in the first column. Add them all up and enter the total outgoings figure at the bottom of that first column.

Then transfer the **Total receipts** figure under the **Summary** heading. Next enter the total **Outgoings** and subtract the Outgoings from the Receipts figure. If the Outgoings figure is higher than the Receipts figure, the excess should be entered as a minus figure. If the latter is the case, see if you can raise any additional funds from any source and enter those figures under the appropriate heading in the middle column.

If you still have a minus figure, go through all the **Expenditure** items numbered 1 to 14, and note down all those which could be reduced or eliminated and enter the lower figures in the appropriate boxes until the **Total expenditure** is less than the **Total receipts**. You need to try to maintain that status quo until you have a regular income again.

Budgeting

Budget period

Receipts	Current income (all sources)	Additional income (sources/amounts)	Comments
1. Net salary			
2. Interest/Dividends			
3. Other amounts			
Total receipts			

Outgoings	Current regular expenditure	Lower amounts you could pay instead	
1. Mortgage/Rent			
2. Endowment and other insurance premiums			
3. Loans/HP/Credit Cards etc.			
4. Clothes for self and family			
5. Motoring costs			
6. Household (heating, electricity etc.)			
7. Gardening			
8. Housekeeping (food and drink etc)			
9. Dependants			
10. Holidays			
11. Personal needs			
12. Job search			
13. Social			
14. Miscellaneous			
Total outgoings			
SUMMARY			
Total receipts			
Total outgoings			
Closing balance			

Summary

When it comes to moving on, the key point is that you have to be aware of your feelings, motives and emotions. In all probability what you are feeling, from elation to depression, is actually normal. Don't give up and do have faith in yourself.

Be clear about why you want to move on and have a vision of where you want to be. Many of the people we have helped in the past have actually said that being made redundant was the best thing that had happened to them, although they probably did not feel that way at the time.

To some extent it is an attitude of mind. Being suddenly unemployed can be seen as an opportunity; a time to review where you want to be and a chance to reflect. Think about what really motivates you in your job and *seek employment where the motivators can be maximized.*

SUNDAY
MONDAY
TUESDAY
WEDNESDAY
THURSDAY
FRIDAY
SATURDAY

Fact-check (answers at the back)

1. In your exit interview you should:
   a) Tell the representative what you really think about how the company has treated you ❏
   b) Use it as an opportunity to get things off your chest ❏
   c) Leave on the best possible terms ❏
   d) Point out that it was not your fault and blame the personality of your line manager ❏

2. When leaving a job, you reflect on the reasons:
   a) So you can blame the company ❏
   b) So you can open your mind to the possibility that it was actually the wrong job for you in the first place ❏
   c) In order to realize that you are a victim ❏
   d) You do not reflect on your reasons for leaving ❏

3. What are your feelings about leaving a job or being forced to leave a job?
   a) You adopt problem-solving behaviour ❏
   b) It is normal to feel optimistic all the time ❏
   c) You direct your aggressive feelings towards others ❏
   d) You blame yourself for losing your job ❏

4. How do you cope with stress?
   a) Direct energy into aggression ❏
   b) Ignore tiredness – bury yourself in work ❏
   c) Sit around and try to relax ❏
   d) Take some physical exercise ❏

5. How do you manage your feelings?
   a) Recognize that your feelings should be suppressed ❏
   b) Assume that being excessively tired is a sure sign of illness ❏
   c) Do not take physical exercise as it will make you feel worse ❏
   d) Do take physical exercise as it can lead to more realistic thoughts ❏

6. Reflect on why you have been made redundant:
   a) It is nothing to do with you personally ❏
   b) It is because you were too good for the organization ❏
   c) It can happen for a multitude of reasons, both economic and personal ❏
   d) It is because your contribution was recognized and valued ❏

7. When you are between jobs:
a) You should review your strengths and weaknesses ❏
b) You shouldn't sign up for any training or retraining courses ❏
c) You should automatically look for work similar to your previous career ❏
d) Brush aside the opportunities and threats that might exist ❏

8. When looking for your next job, you should:
a) Accept any job going ❏
b) Wait around for the perfect job opportunity ❏
c) Discuss your strengths and weaknesses with colleagues and friends ❏
d) Get disheartened by rejections ❏

9. If you see a suitable job advertised you should:
a) Expect to be interviewed within a week ❏
b) Instantly send out your CV without changing it with reference to the job description ❏
c) Not apply because it is less pay than your previous job ❏
d) Expect at least three to four weeks to pass after the advertisement appears before a decision is taken about who is to get the job ❏

10. How do you think about a forthcoming job interview?
a) You do not stand a chance but you will go along anyway ❏
b) You see all interviews as a learning opportunity ❏
c) The prospective employer is very lucky that you are available ❏
d) The interviewer is bound to select the perfect candidate ❏

SUNDAY

MONDAY

TUESDAY

WEDNESDAY

THURSDAY

FRIDAY

SATURDAY

MONDAY

The curriculum vitae or resumé

Today is all about how to research, prepare and write a curriculum vitae (CV) or resumé. The CV needs to be a sales document. You are selling yourself and your knowledge, skills, aptitudes, abilities and experience to potential employers. As in all sales situations, the buyer (the employer) needs to have as much key information about you as possible to enable him/her to decide if you are worth interviewing and whether you will fit into the team and be a productive and valuable member of it.

Therefore, the CV needs to sum up everything about you and your career to date in as persuasive language as possible. It needs to be contained within three pages maximum, ideally, two pages, and should make you sound just right for the position for which you are applying.

SUNDAY

MONDAY

TUESDAY

WEDNESDAY

THURSDAY

FRIDAY

SATURDAY

CV: basics

A good CV (resumé) should describe responsibilities, development, promotions, achievements, knowledge, skills, aptitudes and experience and it needs to relate all of these to the environments in which they occurred. In other words, brief details of the size of the organizations for which you have worked (number of employees, annual revenue [turnover], nature of products/services) and, maybe, why you left. This enables potential new employers to obtain a rounded view of you and the context of your working life.

The purpose of a CV is to enable you to market yourself effectively. It is the individual's equivalent of a brochure of products or services. Like a brochure, presentation is important. It needs to be 'easy on the eye', simple to follow and understand. The CV should contain all of the essential information an employer will need in order to ascertain your suitability for interview. The document also needs to be short and ideally no longer than two pages. Anything more than three pages is unlikely to be read.

Your CV is your opportunity to market yourself

Employers who regularly recruit, frequently receive large numbers of CVs every week. It is important that yours stands out from the rest and contains the most appropriate information on the first page. Like a sales brochure, a CV needs to sell its product – YOU! So you must think of yourself as a product or commodity, identify your strengths and then describe these in such a way as to make interviewing you compelling.

Most employers want people who can do things: **people of action** who **get things done**. So the language you use in your CV needs to reflect these requirements, persuade the recruiters to want to read it and also make interviewing you irresistible.

Your CV needs to be set out logically in short sections and paragraphs with plenty of 'white' space and should **contain everything** that is significant about you and your background. Choosing the words and phrases to use is therefore especially important. Although the purpose of the CV is to sell you, the prime aim is to **secure an interview** to enable you to sell yourself face-to-face.

The information in the CV needs to **tempt the employer** so that an interview invitation follows its submission. You may need to have more than one CV. If your knowledge and skills have been gained in a variety of different jobs or circumstances, you may need to have a different CV for each. However, the common factor with all of them will be layout, presentation and content. Some CVs are very 'wordy'.

The best CVs are concise, straightforward and appropriately written

Opinions differ as to how many main sections a CV should have. You will certainly need to cover personal details; academic and professional qualifications; a career summary; experience and achievements plus training and development.

If you are seeking your first job, think about ways in which you have distinguished yourself at school, college or university. For example, have you held any offices such as being a prefect, team captain in sports or gained prizes or awards of any sort?

Layout and content

Remembering the two-page rule, your CV needs to be concise, dynamic and appealing, but a long career may need more space. So, if you have been at work for 30 years or more, you are going to need to concentrate most of the job-related information in the most recent 15 years or so and therefore the information in this part will be longer than the earlier jobs (see the Rumple Stiltksin example later in this chapter). On the other hand, if the most relevant experience and knowledge for a particular job were one or two jobs back, extend that information in your CV even if it is much longer than more recent experience.

Personal details

These should include your name in capitals and preferably in bold; address, including post code; home phone or mobile phone number and email address. Date of birth and marital status are no longer imperative but may be significant in some roles. Confirmation of driving licence and citizenship could be relevant if you are applying for an international job with an overseas employer or if you were born outside the UK. If you require and hold a work permit, include details of that here too.

Education and qualifications

Enter details of academic achievement and just show the total number of passes at the appropriate level(s) (e.g. 'GCSE: 9 passes and 2 'A' levels). If you do not possess any academic qualifications, do not have a heading for them, otherwise you will have to have a negative entry! Describe also details of higher or further education and the results.

Professional qualifications should be shown separately, including details of professional institution memberships and ability or skill with software packages and foreign languages plus level(s) of ability.

Prospective employers are primarily interested in what you can offer them. So, on the first page of your CV, you should have a summary describing your most significant knowledge, skills, aptitudes and experience. These can be expanded under the headings of the organizations with which you have worked under your Experience and Achievements heading. To some extent this is more important than the organizations for which you have worked. Your experience and achievements may be a short paragraph or, as in our second model CV, nearly a whole page.

Career summary

By summarizing your experience and achievements a prospective employer can see quickly and early on page one whether or not you are the type of person they are looking for. A brief summary of your working life, emphasizing key knowledge, skills and experience serves to whet an employer's appetite for what is to follow in greater detail.

We are describing just two types of CV in this book. First, there is the traditional approach which incorporates a 'Career summary', under your personal details, giving a very brief overview of your employment to date, main abilities and key attributes and achievements. It should contain a descriptive summary of five or six lines followed by a similar number of bullet points. The second type of CV is merely a summary but the first page contains comprehensive details of the precise knowledge, skills and experience tightly related to the vacancy advertised.

If you are applying for an advertised job, ensure you have the written 'Job description/Person profile' in front of you in order to cross/match with the advertisement what you are offering against what is required. This is very important because the larger employers and recruiters frequently use computers to scan CVs first for key words which appear in a job advertisement, job description and candidate personal profiles sought.

Underline or highlight the **key words** and ensure that those which are applicable to your own background appear in your 'Career summary'. Try to describe your knowledge, skills and experience using similar sorts of words to those used by the employer/recruiter in the job advertisement or vacancy information given online (see the Rumple Stiltskin CV).

Experience and achievements

You need to show the dates you joined and left each employer; the last, or most recent position you held and the employer's name. It is also useful to provide some indication as to the organization's size and what it does. Size is indicated by employee numbers and annual financial turnover.

All of these requirements eat into the available space on the page and, if you have access to a PC, one solution is to use a smaller point size for this subsidiary information or type it in *italics* (see the Rumple Stiltskin CV which illustrates these requirements). Recruiters may have dozens (or hundreds) of CVs to consider, when assembling the provisional interview shortlist, and will therefore not want to spend long on each one. It is therefore important that yours presents all the requisite information in a clear, concise and logical sequence.

Your CV should be tailored to your own requirements but also meet the needs of the position for which you are applying. For this reason, it may be wise to have more than one version of your CV so you can emphasize particular strengths which might not be applicable to every job for which you apply. You need to describe your principal responsibilities and your achievements and to qualify and quantify as many as you can which will be significant to the potential employer.

To do this really effectively, try to use verbs which impart a sense of urgency, action and dynamism. These words are given added emphasis if you begin paragraphs and sentences with them and do not use the first persons singular or plural

('I' or 'we'). Instead begin with the participle. Useful participles of verbs to employ, which demonstrate dynamic action, include those listed below.

Dynamic participles

Accessed	Conducted	Examined	Led
Achieved	Constructed	Executed	Liaised
Acquired	Contacted	Expanded	Maintained
Advised	Contracted	Fabricated	Made
Analysed	Contributed	Focused	Managed
Applied	Controlled	Found	Marketed
Appraised	Co-operated	Generated	Mediated
Approved	Co-ordinated	Governed	Monitored
Arranged	Corresponded	Grouped	Motivated
Assembled	Counselled	Guided	Negotiated
Assessed	Created	Identified	Ordered
Assisted	Decided	Implemented	Operated
Bought	Defined	Improved	Organized
Briefed	Delegated	Increased	Originated
Brought	Demonstrated	Informed	Oversaw
Built	Designed	Initiated	Participated
Calculated	Detailed	Inspected	Persuaded
Catalogued	Developed	Inspired	Planned
Checked	Directed	Installed	Prepared
Classified	Drafted	Instilled	Presented
Coached	Edited	Instituted	Processed
Combined	Encouraged	Instructed	Procured
Communicated	Engineered	Interpreted	Produced
Compiled	Erected	Introduced	Programmed
Completed	Established	Investigated	Progressed
Conceived	Estimated	Judged	Promoted

$\longrightarrow$

Prompted	Researched	Sold	Transferred
Protected	Resolved	Solved	Translated
Provided	Reviewed	Strove	Transmitted
Recorded	Revised	Summarized	Transported
Recruited	Revisited	Supervised	Travelled
Rectified	Scheduled	Taught	United
Refocused	Scrutinized	Terminated	Utilized
Regulated	Secured	Tested	Worked
Reported	Selected	Trained	Wrote

The dynamic verbs describe what you **did** but you also need to show what you **achieved** while doing them. The achievements should be qualified or quantified or both.

Look at the Rumple Stiltskin CV below and consider the following examples:

- Under Freshwater Treatment Services Ltd, the last sentence reads: *'... secured agreements from many of the larger PLCs...'*.
- Under Hydroflash UK Limited experience reads: *'Increased sales turnover by 65%'*.
- Under V A Howell & Company Limited: *'Sustained success in sales resulted in consistent career development.'*
- Under International Biograde Ltd: *'Established new distribution centres in the Far East, Australasia, Scandinavia and Europe. Increased sales by 47%.'*
- Under Davis & Gecko Ltd: *'Came 3rd out of 15 sales staff and consistently exceeded targets.'*

These are all achievements which have been either qualified and/or quantified. You should try to show yours in a similar way.

Although achievements are important, so too are other factors such as how you have **added value** for your previous employers through your work and working as a **member of a team** or as a **team leader. Team skills** and experience are nearly always in demand so **mention these every time.**

Experience of involvement in **managing** or **experiencing change** can be significant too and, especially so, if you have led it and see change as a positive challenge. All these need to be described under the appropriate jobs in your CV.

Training and development

It is useful for an employer to know the extent to which you have been trained and developed in each of your jobs. Therefore it is important to list just those programmes which are the **most relevant to the position** for which you are being considered. Again, the Rumple Stiltskin CV shows one approach. Another is to show the years in which the training took place and, especially, if they were during the last ten years or so.

Preparing your own CV

Your employment history should be presented in chronological order; that is, most recent (or current) job first and then earlier ones in reverse date order back to your first one (see the Rumple Stiltskin CV).

The second approach describes in detail your abilities and achievements and how you have added value to your previous jobs. This could cover the most of page one of your CV, the other page is just a one line descriptive summary about the previous employers you have worked for, the dates you joined and left and your most recent job title with each (see the Jack Horner CV).

The advantage of this approach is that the prospective employer can see on page one whether or not you are the type of person they are looking for. If your 'Abilities and achievements' are what they seek, then they will read on to find out about your previous employers and earlier roles. This is especially useful when you are applying for a vacancy where your knowledge, skills and experience are particularly apposite. In this situation, your abilities and achievements summary can give you a real edge when being considered by a busy recruiter. This is because all the critical information appears on the first page.

SUNDAY
MONDAY
TUESDAY
WEDNESDAY
THURSDAY
FRIDAY
SATURDAY

The second page is merely the briefest summary of the appointments you have held and your qualifications. At an interview, you can produce the full CV version (e.g. Rumple Stiltskin type of layout) if appropriate. Much consideration needs to be taken with the descriptions of your abilities. They must be chosen carefully from what may be a very full and successful career. Select those of particular relevance to the position for which you are applying. The same degree of attention must be taken too with the achievements selected as being appropriate. A starting point for both could be your written Job Description(s) and appraisal documentation, if you have access to them.

Note the use of emotive and dynamic verbs and phrases used in the Jack Horner CV to **wring maximum meaning** and **impact** from the words used. This approach is particularly useful when you can demonstrate in a few words the range and depth of your relevant knowledge, skills and achievements. It is obvious that you really know what you are talking about.

The quality and colour of paper used for the CV is important too. The thicker (and heavier) it is, the greater the psychological impact of quality on the holder of the document. Heavier paper (like Conqueror or Bond) of 120 gsm feels more substantial and imparts an impression of quality which can reflect favourably on you. Product advertisers use quality materials on which to describe their wares in much the same way and so should you. Obviously, if applying online, paper quality is irrelevant!

The two CV examples discussed here (Rumple Stiltskin and Jack Horner) follow below. Owing to the size of the pages in this book, it is not possible to illustrate the layout of the CVs in the manner described here. However, a number of examples can be found by visiting www.fresh-fields.com.

The Rumple Stiltksin CV supports applying for a job in senior management and the Jack Horner CV supports applying for a job in training management. Sample CVs for jobs at other levels can also be seen at www.fresh-fields.com.

Rumple STILTSKIN

8 Wareham Lane Epping Essex WM3 7BX

Phone 0181 963 7351 Mobile 07778 942635

Email Rumple@Stiltskin.co.uk

Education and qualifications

Academic Achievement	GCE: 9 'O' levels; 4 'A' levels & 1 'S' level
Higher Education	BSc Applied Biology, London University
Professional	MBA from the Business School at Kingston
Software Skills	Excel, Access, Word, Outlook and PowerPoint

Career summary

A sales and marketing professional with general management experience, underpinned with a Masters in Business Administration (MBA), who has provided front-line consultancy support to chief executives and human resources professionals in organizations ranging in size from 50 to thousands of employees. This experience has been achieved within the framework of the Investors in People national Standard as both a qualified Adviser and Assessor approved by the Chartered Institute of Personnel & Development.

- Over 20 years' sales and marketing experience with 14 of them in management roles.
- Comprehensive experience in man-management and in devising, implementing and controlling sales and marketing plans and budgets within the UK and export remits.
- Customer base has included central government departments, educational, commercial, industrial, research and business to business markets.
- Demonstrable success in planning and managing change and in producing significant sales growth.
- Substantial experience in advising and assessing organizations of diverse sizes against acknowledged national and international Quality Standards.

Experience and achievements

1993 – Present Sales Manager – Wessex Learning & Skills Council
The LSC provides advice on training, funding and opportunities to individuals & organizations via a range of government programmes/ initiatives including Investors in People. It has 60 employees & a turnover/operating budget of £24 million.

Primary accountability is to secure 'commitments' to the Investors in People national quality Standard from organizations with 50+ employees and to manage the same through to 'recognition'. Responsible for a team of eight, comprising Key Account Managers and admin support. Advise own accounts through diagnosis, action-planning and implementation through to assessment. Also assess organizations myself against the national Standard. Under my leadership, the team has consistently achieved or exceeded targets in a demanding environment of constant change and uncertainty.

Water treatment company manufacturing and supplying equipment and chemicals to prevent corrosion, scaling and Legionella risks in all sizes of UK water systems. There were 70 employees and turnover of £3.6 million.

Introduced a marketing strategy and controls for Middle East and European export activities of the water treatment products and services. Designed and produced new literature and introduced computer-based marketing approaches. Responsible for key accounts and secured agreements from many of the larger PLCs to enable the company to tender for their business.

1990–1992 Managing Director – Hydroflash UK Limited
UK distributor of electronic water treatment equipment for the reduction of hard water scaling in large capacity and domestic water systems. Wholly owned subsidiary of the Berkeley Group plc. Nine employees and £775,000 turnover.

Reorganized this water treatment company, establishing protocols and objectives. Responsible for the day-to-day management of the company. Introduced computer-based databases and sales prospecting programs to focus sales and marketing activities. Increased sales turnover by 65%.

1987–1989 Business Manager – International Biograde Limited
Manufacturer of biological products for use in waste water systems to degrade pollutants. Products sold world-wide via distributors. 100 employees based in Dublin, Slough & USA.

Responsible for the worldwide planning and management of the sales and marketing of the Waste Water Treatment Division's pollution control products for all countries with the exception of North America. Researched, designed and introduced new literature, marketing and training aids to support distributors. Established new distribution centres in the Far East, Australasia, Scandinavia & Europe. Increased sales by 47%.

1977–1987 Sales Director – V A Howell and Company Limited
Privately owned distributor of scientific and medical instrumentation and consumables imported from USA, Japan & Europe. Employees numbered 100 and turnover was £6 million.

During ten years of employment with the company, was promoted three times. Joined as Product Specialist and progressed through Divisional Sales Management to Group Sales Manager (two years) and finally to the Board as Sales Director (also two years). Designed and introduced sales prospecting, reporting programs and new commission schemes for sales staff; profitability targets for managers and appraisal systems. Sustained success in sales resulted in consistent career development.

1976–1977 Salesman/Product Specialist – GoldStraw plc
The Factored Instrument Division was a UK distributor of scientific and medical products from USA and Europe and was wholly owned by the GoldStraw Group. 100 employees.

Promotion from Salesman to Product Specialist came at the end of the first year as a result of substantially exceeding budgeted sales figures and achieving Top Salesman within the factored scientific and medical products division.

1973–1976 Salesman – Davis & Gecko Ltd
Manufacturer of surgical sutures for use in wound closure. Wholly owned by Gecko Corporation.

As a result of exceeding budgeted sales of surgical sutures to hospital consultants and other appropriate staff, was promoted to cover the London Teaching Hospitals. Came 3rd out of 15 sales staff and consistently exceeded targets. Responsible for training new staff and presenting seminars.

1972–1973 Analytical Chemist – Wyte and Brother
Manufacturers of pharmaceutical products.

Analysed new and existing pharmaceutical formulations for quality and content using a wide range of analytical techniques.

Training courses attended

Finance for Non-financial Managers	4 days
Marketing Planning (Cranfield)	2 days
Export Marketing (Chartered Institute of Marketing)	2 days
Negotiating Contracts (Dunn & Bradstreet)	1 day
Microsoft Word	1 day
Outlook and PowerPoint	1 day
360° Appraisal Skills for Managers	2 days

JACK HORNER
70 Hazel Road Barley-on-Medway Kent BK8 8HR
Phone 01239 874567 Mobile 07778 123654
Email jack@plumpud.co.uk

ABILITIES

- Provide a complete staff training and management development facility.
- Carry out training needs analyses, identify what needs to be done and prioritize.
- Research, design and present training events using own and external resources.
- Set standards and objectives, measure outcomes and follow up as necessary.
- Prepare budget forecasts, negotiate for same and maintain expenditure accounts.
- Establish and maintain training records and liaise internally and externally.
- Market all training facilities and maximize efficient and profitable use.
- Research applications, write scripts and produce video films.
- Formulate or contribute to corporate training & development philosophy and policy.
- Train people of all ages regardless of learning ability, employment status, cultural or social background.
- Lead by example, inspire confidence, instill enthusiasm and commitment through the provision of training which is creative and stimulating, challenging yet supportive but always participative.

ACHIEVEMENTS

- Successfully introduced and maintained the Japanese style of management with an all-British workforce through employee participation and involvement. Drew favourable comments from the management press and presented public courses on Total Quality Management (TQM).
- Designed, wrote, produced and co-directed a series of product knowledge video films. Raised product knowledge internally as well as with retail clients' sales teams. This paid for production costs and also directly, and measurably, increased overall corporate profitability by 15%.
- Refocused entrenched negative attitudes of long-serving, middle managers to change. Provided stimulation and remotivation through counselling and training and proved that old dogs can learn new tricks and enjoy applying them.
- Encouraged all personnel to study for professional qualifications with dramatic results. Professional institute memberships increased more than tenfold in four years.
- HR managers complained that line management made poor recruitment decisions, overlooked the best candidates and, when they did pick them, could not keep them. Introduced interviewing, leadership, communication, delegation, motivation, coaching, time management and counselling skills training for managers combined with liaison and customer care training for non-supervisory staff. Morale soared, staff turnover was halved and customer complaints fell sharply.
- Brought in Team Briefing, overcoming stiff senior management resistance through persuasion. Later surveyed all personnel and results confirmed success of the briefing programme through enhanced job satisfaction and achievement of individual, team and overall company goals and targets on time and within budgets.

SUNDAY MONDAY TUESDAY WEDNESDAY THURSDAY FRIDAY SATURDAY

WORK HISTORY

1995–Present	Business Partner – Goodboy Management Consultancy
1992–1995	Investors in People Key Account Manager – Wessex TEC
1987–1991	Training Manager – First Cleveland Bank Plc
1984–1987	Management Consultant – Team Training International
1981–1984	Administrative Services Manager – Triangle Inc International
1973–1981	Personnel/Group Training Manager – Plantation (UK) Ltd
1969–1973	Section Leader – Comical Magical & Genial Life Assurance
1968–1969	General Manager – Victoria Hotel, Torquay
1959–1968	German Linguist – Royal Air Force (Intelligence Branch)
1957–1959	New Business Clerk – MPI Life Assurance Institution

EDUCATIONAL and PROFESSIONAL QUALIFICATIONS

GCE 'O' and 'A' levels including Maths and English

Civil Service Commission Languages Board – German Linguist

City & Guilds 730 – Further and Adult Education Teacher's Certificate

Chartered Institute of Personnel and Development – Investors in People Assessor

Chartered Institute of Personnel & Development – Member (MCIPD)

Henley Distance Learning (Investors in People) – Levels 2, 3A & 3B

City & Guilds – Vocational & Skills Assessor (NVQ Units D32/D33)

Chartered Institute of Marketing – Member (MCIM)

The Law Society – Lexcel Adviser and Assessor

Summary

We have examined the CV in depth, its purpose, layout, content, order of headings and overall presentational impact. A really good CV needs to stand out and content is critical. There is an old military acronym which is relevant to CVs. It is KISS – Keep It Simple, (Stupid)! CVs have come a long way in the last 30 years and some now are submitted in PowerPoint formats with music and animation. However, the vast majority still arrive in the format described above.

SUNDAY
MONDAY
TUESDAY
WEDNESDAY
THURSDAY
FRIDAY
SATURDAY

Fact-check (answers at the back)

1. What is the main purpose of a CV?
   a) To enable you to look good on paper ❏
   b) To impress your family and friends ❏
   c) To make your work history look more respectable ❏
   d) To enable you to market yourself more effectively ❏

2. What attributes do most employers hope applicants will possess?
   a) Look presentable ❏
   b) Ability to do things well and get them done ❏
   c) Live nearby and will arrive for work punctually ❏
   d) Good sickness absence record. ❏

3. What is the prime aim of a CV?
   a) To get you a good salary and fringe benefits ❏
   b) To help you remember better what you did in the past ❏
   c) To secure an interview ❏
   d) To secure the job ❏

4. How would you describe your strengths and achievements?
   a) Modestly ❏
   b) Using simple words ❏
   c) Using upward-sounding dynamic words ❏
   d) Using words that exaggerate your achievements ❏

5. Which personal details should you provide?
   a) Name, address, landline and mobile phone numbers and email address, date of birth, marriage status and number of children ❏
   b) First name and surname, address, landline and mobile phone numbers, email address. ❏
   c) Name, address, phone number(s), email address, age, clean driving licence ❏
   d) Names and address, landline and mobile phone numbers, email address, names and addresses of two referees and how long they've known me. ❏

6. What information about present and past employers should be in your CV?
   a) The names of previous employers from last to first, last/present job title, dates joined and left, number of staff in organization and annual turnover, nature of business ❏
   b) The names of the companies worked for and what they did ❏
   c) School leaving dates, details of first job, followed by subsequent jobs ❏
   d) A list of what you did in your work for each organization ❏

7. In what order should your work history be shown?

a) In date order – your first job first and your most recent job last ❏

b) In no particular order ❏

c) In alphabetical order of the initial letters of the names of the companies ❏

d) In chronological order – your most recent job first and your first job last ❏

8. Into how much detail should you go concerning your academic qualifications?

a) List the subjects and grades in the order that you passed them ❏

b) Give the number of passes at the various common levels ❏

c) List school exam passes by subject and show college/university results after ❏

d) If aged under 25, list school/college passes by subject and grade. If over 25, just give the number of passes at the appropriate levels ❏

9. How should you describe your achievements?

a) For each job you have had, describe your main targets and how you met them ❏

b) Just write down what you did well ❏

c) Describe your main responsibilities and how you performed them ❏

d) Qualify your main achievements and quantify the outcomes ❏

10. What activities within your work experience are most likely to impress a new employer?

a) Your attendance record and general good behaviour at work ❏

b) Being popular with colleagues and management ❏

c) Adding value, having team skills and enthusiastically embracing change ❏

d) A willingness to welcome new people and help them settle in ❏

TUESDAY

Marketing yourself

You have researched, designed and written your CV and now it is time to use it as an effective tool to get interviews. If it is going to be really effective you need to know yourself really well. When marketing ourselves, we should be keenly aware of our Strengths and Weaknesses, Opportunities and Threats. Today we are going to do just that. On the basis of the results, we should have a better idea of ourselves, the sort of people we are, the type of work at which we should excel and the sort of openings to avoid.

Seeing a job change as an opportunity

One of the best methods for coping with a job change is to see the advantages of the space between jobs. To some extent this is an attitude of mind – looking at the bottle as being half-full rather than half-empty. The opportunities could be as follows:

- If you are happy in your present career, then at least you know the type of job you are looking for. If you have doubts about your present career, then *take time out to find out what type of career you would really like*. Discover as much as you can about this new career and then look at your strengths. You may not have the correct qualifications or the normal career path but you may have the right work experience, aptitude and enthusiasm. These attributes combined with your work record could impress an employer more than letters after your name.
- If you have the financial means, such as redundancy money, you could consider starting a **short educational or occupational course** to obtain the relevant **qualifications or skills**. If you land a suitable job before the course finishes, you can always study part-time or in the evenings. Signing up to an appropriate skills or qualifications programme goes down well with any future employer as it shows commitment.

Write down all your strengths and skills and then **brainstorm what other avenues these strengths and skills can be used for**. Try to think 'outside the box'. You are an experienced manager, an experienced leader. You are self-disciplined and flexible. Don't take your work experience for granted and do try to learn to psychologically re-package yourself.

Being between jobs gives you the **opportunity to network** with all your friends and acquaintances and their friends and acquaintances so that they can look around for relevant opportunities in their organizations and networks. By discussing your aspirations with others, they may be able to identify other appropriate openings in different sectors that you may not have considered or of which you may even be unaware.

Identifying personal strengths and weaknesses

A very simple method of preparing yourself for your next job is to conduct your own SWOT analysis. 'SWOT' stands for individual **Strengths** and **Weaknesses** and the external **Opportunities** and **Threats.**

Strengths and weaknesses

The simplest method is to sit down with two pieces of paper, one headed 'Strengths' and the other headed 'Weaknesses'. Start off with your strengths and write them down (these are all the things at which you excel). At the same time, you might find that you also identify your weaknesses, so write them down as well. The strengths and weaknesses that we are concerned with are those related to your last job or the sort of job for which you would like to apply. Occupational competencies, relevant to your strengths and weaknesses, occur under three broad headings:

- Professional and technical competencies
- Systems and procedural competencies
- Intra-personal and team competencies

Take time to identify your strengths, however hidden they might be

Professional and technical

Professional competencies are those linked to qualifications or to being a member of a professional association. Management comes under the term 'Professional competence' because it is not really a technical skill but is seen as 'professional', although you can practise management without belonging to a professional body.

Technical competencies are the skills associated with a job, such as operating a computer, accountancy, sales, using a particular software package, operating a forklift truck, etc. Technical competencies are often acquired through experience and are to do with skills and knowledge.

Systems and procedural

These differ from organization to organization, and so we need not look at our strengths and weaknesses around these competencies. They are only important when we have been offered the job. 'Systems and procedures' are to do with the rules, regulations and processes found in all organizations, e.g. health and safety, IT, working practices, quality procedures and so on.

Intra-personal and team

Intra-personal competencies are about how you manage yourself, such as time management, decision making and prioritizing. Team competencies are concerned with your interests, aptitudes and experiences when working with others. Do you enjoy working in teams? Do you like being a team leader? Do you have good intra-personal skills and can you deal with difficult people or awkward customers? Some jobs are suited to those who have the interpersonal skills associated with teamwork; other jobs may have less reliance on team working.

List your strengths

The idea is to brainstorm all your skills, experience, training, education, professional institution memberships, aptitudes, interests, hobbies, membership of clubs and societies and so on. Many people have acquired skills and knowledge that they take for granted. A good example of this is when women return to work when their children go to school. Such women in the past have described themselves as merely a 'housewife' when, in fact, their knowledge and experience is concerned with bringing up children, managing the household, budgeting and so on.

If you have the results of any psychometric tests, especially those to do with career interests, aptitudes, skills or team roles, you can use these results as part of your strength profile. You can edit the test results so that you leave out the weaknesses and concentrate only on the positive profile. By brainstorming all your skills and experience, whether professionally recognized or not, you can build up an image of your STRENGTHS – i.e. those competencies you can offer a new employer.

It is your strengths that appear on page one of the CV and you bring out in the interview.

List your weaknesses

When looking at your professional/technical skills and interpersonal/team skills, and thinking about the jobs you would like to do, you should identify your relevant WEAKNESSES. *These are the competencies that you lack for the job in question.* Your list of weaknesses is for your eyes only; you make the list to help you understand yourself.

There are two types of weakness. The first weakness is the lack of experience or knowledge of a particular area, *but you may feel you have the aptitude to learn* that skill or acquire that knowledge. The second concerns those skill areas that *do not interest you and for which you do not have the aptitude*. If a particular job requires mostly skills associated with this second form of weakness, then the job is not for you and you would be unhappy working in that area. If there are small parts of a job that contain areas which do not suit your aptitudes, most of us can acquire the skills to cope with them.

When it comes to weaknesses that are really due to a lack of experience or training, *but you feel you have the aptitude*, then you must see this area as a weakness *that you need to do something about*. There are two actions you can take, which are not mutually exclusive:

● First, if you have the time and resources, you can **train yourself** while looking for a job. This training could be by distance learning, the Open University, evening classes, or through the internet, etc. It is always a good sign to a prospective employer that you have recognized a weakness and are doing something about it.

- The second action is to **mention the limit of experience** (do not use the word weakness) in the interview itself, or on the application form, and say that you are interested in being trained in that area, or that you are willing to train yourself. Employers appreciate a candidate being open about their strengths and 'lack of experience' as it indicates an understanding of the job and also a degree of self-awareness.

Opportunities and threats

Opportunities

Once you have examined your strengths and weaknesses you can now look at the opportunities and threats that present themselves. Opportunities really arise from looking at your strengths and aptitudes, *as it is these that direct you to your next job*. You must always remember that your strengths and aptitudes could be applied outside the industry where you have the most experience.

For example, many skills are transferable between very different occupations. One client had been a hairdresser and wanted to work in an office instead. She successfully applied for a job in the Facilities Management office in a firm of solicitors. Dealing with people on the phone and face-to-face; having a positive outlook; being welcoming and putting people at their ease; handling electrical machinery. All these skills apply to hairdressing and office facilities management!

If you are intending to seek a new career, then examine whether or not the industry or sector has a future. It is unwise to seek a job that is in a declining demand or an industry that is downsizing.

In times of full employment, there are clearly more job opportunities around and you should seek out those jobs best suited to your interests, experience and remunerative needs. When national economies are in recession, it may take longer to find a suitable job. In many cases finding the job you want will be easier if you can be flexible. Flexibility comes in various forms:

Income flexibility

It is not wise to go for a job, similar to the one you are now in, with an income far lower than your previous role, unless you have no alternative. On the other hand, a job with an income of £2,000 pa lower than your previous salary, or a job with no company car, may not substantially affect your standard of living, especially if you take into account the tax you have to pay. Those who have been offered an early retirement package, or a pension but who still need to work, can probably afford to be employed in lower income jobs if necessary.

It can also be worth looking at some lower paid jobs *if they have training opportunities or have the prospect of promotion or career enhancement*. Quality of life can be more important than a high salary. A slight fall in salary may be worth it if you will be happier in the new role. Generally speaking, people are more likely to accept lower pay if it is a change of career. They are less likely to accept lower pay if it is the same type of job in the same sector.

Flexibility and an openness to all possibilities can turn weaknesses into strengths

Geographical flexibility

Being able to move house, or being willing to travel further to your place of work, increases your opportunities. Your partner's job or the children's education may prevent this form of flexibility. The cost of moving needs to be taken into account and also the prices of houses in the area to which you might move. A lower cost area increases your disposable income so your standard of living might go up even if your gross income falls slightly.

Occupational flexibility

It has become much more acceptable, and in some cases is seen as an advantage, to change careers completely.

Individuals with more than one career are often seen as more experienced and more employable. Engineers with good people skills might move into training, education or human resource management. Craftsmen might become self-employed contractors. Senior managers might move into consultancy and car mechanics might find better career prospects in the local production plant.

If you are in the fortunate position to find yourself between jobs, you have four clear options:

1 Find a similar job in a similar type of organization.
2 Find a similar job in a different type of organization.
3 Find a different job in a similar type of organization.
4 Find a completely different job in a different type of organization.

Threats

There are several threats of which you need to be aware in order to help you make the right decision about your next job.

Threat one

Lack of financial resources may mean a radical change in your lifestyle. If you are unemployed for a length of time, can you afford the mortgage and the other debts you may have? Think the unthinkable and plan for the worst scenario. It will probably never happen but at least you will have prepared yourself.

Threat two

Employers may feel you are too old for the job in question. This has become known as **ageism.** You have talents and experience that organizations actually require, so the real threat is more likely to be the lack of ability to sell yourself. Older people have the advantage of being experienced and seldom want to claw their way up the occupational hierarchy. They therefore seldom present a threat to younger ambitious people.

Threat three

One of the most powerful threats is your own attitude towards unemployment. Optimistic, flexible people are more likely to find work first. The key to success is to know what type of job you want, update and improve your CV and learn the skills of being interviewed. Learn to sell yourself and remain confident.

> ***'We have nothing to fear but fear itself.'***
>
> Franklin D. Roosevelt

As a general rule, there are more job opportunities out there than you might think!

The use of psychometric tests

In your previous job you may have filled in a psychometric test to do with your behaviour at work. Some common ones are: The Belbin Team Role Inventory, Occupational Personality Questionnaire (OPQ32) and the Thomas International Personal Profile Analysis (PPA).

The Belbin test indicates your team role preferences and individuals tend to score high on some preferences and low on others. The test results indicate how you are likely to behave in a team. The OPQ test describes how you relate to people, your thinking style and your feelings and emotions.

The Thomas International test looks at your self-image, how you present yourself in the work role and how you are likely to behave under pressure. The Thomas test looks at things like Dominance, Influence, Steadiness and Compliance.

Some employers use psychometric tests to help in the selection process because they can provide some insight into how people are likely to behave in their next job.

It can be a very useful addition to your CV, or in the interview, to mention your test results if you have them. Employers are more likely to believe the test results than your subjective description of yourself! Read through the test results and pull out those descriptions of your personality that you think would add support to your application. If the test results are very supportive then attach them to your CV as an appendix. If you just mention the odd strength in the CV, that is also fine. For example, 'I came out as a high "Team Worker" in the Belbin test,' or 'In the Thomas International PPA test I scored high on Influencing'. The idea is to mention your strengths if they are supportive of your job application.

Psychometric tests also give you considerable insight into your own strengths and weaknesses. Go for those jobs that build on your strengths as these are the jobs where you are more likely to be fulfilled and successful.

As well as giving you insight into yourself, any psychometric tests you have taken can be a useful addition to your CV

Having identified your strengths and looked at the opportunities, the next stage is to market yourself.

Marketing yourself

Marketing is about presenting yourself to prospective employers. It is the pre-interview preparation. In the interview you are selling yourself. *Marketing is presenting yourself in such a way that the prospective employer wants to interview you.*

Achievements

Prospective employers are not interested in a one-line description of the content of your last job. They want to know what you have **achieved** and how you **added value** to your last employer. How many people were you responsible for? What was the size of your budget? What changes or improvements did you introduce in your last job? Remember that each job has four essential elements that are described under the titles **Maintenance, Crisis Prevention, Continuous Improvement** and the **Management of Change.** (From Ted Johns, of *Perfect Time Management*, Random House, 1995.)

1 Maintenance

These are activities that essentially make up your role, the duties and responsibilities that really describe the job. The maintenance tasks describe what you do, *they do not describe how effective you were or how you added value.*

2 Crisis prevention

In all jobs you learn from mistakes and anticipate things going wrong. Crisis prevention is about being one jump ahead. The flip side of crisis prevention is fire fighting, If you did not carry out the 'crisis prevention' tasks you would be seen as inefficient and more of a liability than an asset.

3 Continuous improvement

These are activities that add value to the organization. It is doing whatever you do quicker, with higher quality, at lower cost etc. Introducing continuous improvement activities is an essential part of most jobs these days and you need to market yourself with reference to the improvements you have introduced to your last job or roles. Expect the astute interviewer to ask you the question, 'How have you improved your job or added value to your job over the last year?'

4 Management of change

These are activities that bring in new ideas, challenge current assumptions and radically change things. The management of change is about whole new processes, finding new and different customers, creating fresh and diverse products and alternative markets. These novel ideas may involve new technology or just completely different ways to do things.

What is important about the management of change is that introducing change is actually more difficult than coming up with the new ideas. To be part of the change process is as important as marketing yourself. Most organizations these days are undergoing change and those people who have the experience of the change process are perceived as more desirable.

To sum up, you can describe yourself by what you do (maintenance and crisis prevention) but you must market yourself on how you have added value (continuous improvement and the management of change). Marketing is about presenting yourself in a positive light and how you can add value to the prospective employer's organization. *The essence of marketing is focusing on your unique selling point (USP) – i.e. what makes you uniquely different from other candidates.*

Summary

Through various analytical methods, the SWOT test and psychometrics, we have examined ourselves, identified our strengths and weaknesses and how to exploit the former and live with the latter. We have also considered steps we can take to improve our chances of identifying and securing work and have reviewed the sort of circumstances which can frustrate us in these endeavours.

We have reviewed our achievements, how we react to change, add value in our work, plan for potential crises and generally conduct ourselves appropriately and safely. Continuous improvement in everything we do in our work is what we should strive to achieve, regularly challenging what we do and seeking ways to do it more quickly, accurately and at less cost.

Success is more likely to result if we can be more flexible in our approaches and we have considered the types of flexibility and the benefits these can produce to smooth our progress back into full employment. The advantages of training, whether in knowledge, skills or experience have been evaluated along with potential outcomes and the possible benefits these may derive.

SUNDAY
MONDAY
TUESDAY
WEDNESDAY
THURSDAY
FRIDAY
SATURDAY

Fact-check (answers at the back)

1. There are three essential elements in all jobs:
   a) Competencies in status, pay and career elements ❏
   b) Competencies in seeking advancement, skill and efficiency ❏
   c) Competencies in professional/technical, systems/procedural and intra-personal/team elements ❏
   d) Competencies in professional, technical and following procedures ❏

2. Effectiveness resides in:
   a) Maintenance – fulfilling the job description ❏
   b) Crisis prevention – being one jump ahead and anticipating errors ❏
   c) Making sure you follow the rules ❏
   d) Continuous improvement and the management of change ❏

3. How can psychometric tests aid us to obtain employment?
   a) Interviewers will be impressed that we spent money on them ❏
   b) They are a useful source of unbiased opinion of our strengths/aptitudes ❏
   c) They look good on a CV ❏
   d) They are never wrong ❏

4. Occupational flexibility means:
   a) Going for the same job in the same industry or sector ❏
   b) Being open to any job in any industry or sector commensurate with one's skills/aptitudes ❏
   c) Being open to any job in any industry or sector irrespective of one's skills and aptitudes ❏
   d) Going to the same type of job in a different location ❏

5. What does 'adding value' mean?
   a) Everything is getting more expensive ❏
   b) We will have to work harder for less money ❏
   c) Trying to improve the quality/output of our work in the same time and at the same cost ❏
   d) Increasing the firm's prices for the services it provides ❏

6. What is the management of change all about?
   a) Making changes and then trying to manage them ❏
   b) Just creating new ideas and challenges ❏
   c) Making do when things go wrong in the office ❏
   d) Challenging the status quo and implementing new ideas in order to improve overall performance ❏

7. What sort of new people do many employers want?
a) People who stir everybody up and change things ❏
b) Those who implement change and embrace it ❏
c) People who maintain the status quo ❏
d) Younger people who are less expensive to employ ❏

8. What is important about the management of change?
a) Once you have the change idea it is easy to implement ❏
b) To shake out those people who can't cope with it and replace them ❏
c) Prepare for change to be resisted so it will have to be managed and that is a skill ❏
d) Everyone has the ability to manage change, it does not require special skills ❏

9. What are the benefits of geographical flexibility?
a) Having a change of scene and meeting new people ❏
b) It provides greater job opportunities ❏
c) A chance to get away from people you dislike ❏
d) You and the family can move house ❏

10. What are the two main types of weakness when seeking employment?
a) Lack of self-confidence and commitment ❏
b) Lack of experience but you have the aptitude or lack of motivation ❏
c) Fear of failure and getting a worse boss ❏
d) Lethargy and low drive ❏

WEDNESDAY

Job search

So far, we have looked at moving on from unemployment, considered our feelings in the circumstances and planned our finances. We have also thought about the future, written a CV and then examined our strengths and weaknesses, reflecting on where we want to go from here, and the sort of work we seek and the knowledge, skills and experience we can bring to a new position. We are now going to look for that job and identify as many opportunities as possible to secure employment (if that is what is sought).

SUNDAY

MONDAY

TUESDAY

WEDNESDAY

THURSDAY

FRIDAY

SATURDAY

Sourcing employment opportunities

There are a variety of ways in which you can source employment opportunities. You can apply for advertised vacancies; try 'prospecting' for employment opportunities by approaching employers and asking if they have any work for you; seek out temporary or freelance work or even unpaid voluntary work. The latter can sometimes result in permanent paid work, for people who show that they are worthy future employees who can be relied upon to make a beneficial contribution.

Traditionally, job-seekers would look through newspapers, business magazines and trade publications for advertised jobs. You can still do this by visiting your local library and looking through all the day's national newspapers, trade magazines and business directories etc. for job advertisements.

Organizations still use traditional media such as newspapers, journals and directories, as well as the internet, to advertise vacancies

However, with the advent of the internet, many of these steps can now be taken without leaving home by accessing them through a computer. Nevertheless, the directories that provide information about companies and public sector organizations are generally too expensive to buy, if you are just looking for work, but libraries do still have them. Two are particularly useful and probably available in the public libraries of most large towns and cities in the UK. These are Kelly's Industrial Directory and Kompass.

The purpose of directories is to use them to identify organizations which may have vacancies for the sort of work that you are seeking. This approach is called 'prospecting'. **You can prospect for jobs** by identifying organizations close to where you live, or want to work, which may employ people doing the sort of work you seek.

Although a large number of public libraries have contracted or disappeared altogether, many do still exist. When you go, ask where the business directories are kept. You can either write down the details of the companies in which you are interested, or you can photocopy the pages which contain the firms you want to contact.

Many libraries also have computer terminals available for customers. Unlike desktop computers and PCs, these can only access the internet. They have printer links and can be cost effective.

Many jobs are advertised by recruitment agencies. The vacancies they handle come from two main sources: they are asked by employers to recruit the people they need or they trawl the internet looking for advertised vacancies placed by employers and then seek candidates for them.

Other sources of employment opportunities are the social media websites like LinkedIn, Facebook, Twitter and the like. Many commercial organizations are members of these and advertise vacancies on their websites. Individuals can also have membership of them and announce to the world the sort of jobs they are seeking and how they are qualified for them. They also network within the social media sites through friends of friends and so on.

Another angle is to try networking with all good friends and acquaintances and give them your business card (inexpensive to buy).

Scan the local newspapers and listen to local radio stations for information about trade fairs and special events. These are often organized by the Chambers of Commerce, Business Links and other organizations promoting employment, apprenticeships and further education opportunities and similar in your area.

Get the financial or business newspapers to see which companies are expanding or have won major contracts. Local or regional newspapers often have articles about local companies or those organizations that might be carrying out a major recruitment drive. *Use this information to acquaint them with your CV.*

Then there is the internet itself. There are huge opportunities there, and below are details of sites you can visit which specialize in advertising employment opportunities. Seek out likely jobs. These are facilitated by search engines such as Google, Yahoo, Ask Jeeves, btinternet, fsnet, aol, totalise, demon and hotmail etc.

Make a start with the websites below, which have been recommended to us in the UK, but remember there are thousands more (millions globally) so we can only give you a flavour of what is available. You will soon find which ones work best for you and you will also discover many more during your own web browsing.

You can use a general CV or resumé for prospecting letters, but may need to have more focused copies for specialist roles where your CV needs to be written specifically to reflect these. The accompanying application letters need appropriate wording too and you must phrase these very carefully. (An example of this appears in the Thursday chapter.) You will also need to set up a system to manage these applications so that you know to whom each was sent, which CV version accompanied the letter and whether they were emailed or posted. We have a control sheet for this purpose which is also in the Thursday section.

General work-related websites in the UK

www.1job.co.uk
3wjobs.com
www.agencycentral.co.uk
www.alljobsuk.com
www.best-people.co.uk
www.britishjobs.net
www.brookstreet.co.uk
www.check4jobs.com
www.CV-Library.co.uk
www.fish4jobs.co.uk
www.gisajob.co.uk

http://jobseekers.direct.gov.uk
http://jobs.guardian.co.uk
www.jobsinwales.com
www.jobsword.co.uk
http://jobs.telegraph.co.uk
www.jobxpress.co.uk
www.manpower.co.uk
www.monster.co.uk
www.randstad.co.uk
www.reed.co.uk
www.royalmail.com

www.hays.com
www.hotrecruit.co.uk
www.jobcentreplus.gov.uk
www.jobhunter.co.uk
www.jobmall.co.uk
www.jobs.co.uk
www.jobs1.co.uk
www.jobsin.co.uk
www.jobsite.co.uk
www.salestarget.co.uk

www.scottishjobs.com
www.stopgap.co.uk
www.thisislondon.co.uk
www.timesonline.co.uk
www.totaljobs.com
www.uk.plusjobs.com
www.workcircle.com
www.workgateways.com
www.workthing.com

Specialist work-related websites

www.afse.org.uk
www.blindinbusiness.org.uk
www.disabledworkers.org.uk
www.internationaljobs.org
www.opportunities.org.uk

www.scope.org.uk
www.careers.lon.ac.uk
www.emjobsite.co.uk
www.talentladder.com

Public-sector job websites

www.emedcareers.co.uk
www.governmentjobsdirect.co.uk
www.healthcarejobs.co.uk
www.jobsgopublic.com
www.jobs.ac.uk/sector/politics
www.lgjobs.com
www.nhsjobs.com
www.publicjobsdirect.com

http://jobs.healthcarerepublic.com
www.healthjobsuk.com
http://www2.nmc4jobs.com
www.fireservice.co.uk
www.policecouldyou.co.uk
www.army.mod.uk
www.raf.mod.uk
www.royal-navy.mod.uk

Networking

The older and more experienced you are, the more likely you are to get a job through networking. Being recommended by another employee is a powerful way in which to get a job.

Give friends and relations your CV and a business card. Tell them what type of job you are looking for and then leave it up to them. There is no harm in doing this as long as you do not apply pressure, as it can be embarrassing.

In your last job you may have established good relationships with customers, suppliers, subcontractors and so on, even competitors. Phone up your contacts and tell them you are in the job market, send them your CV or ask them who is the best person to speak to about roles in their organization. Don't be shy about meeting these people to discuss your situation and also ask them who you should approach there and if you can use your friend's name to get an introduction to an HR or other person handling recruitment.

Cold call companies that you have worked with in the past; get through to the decision makers or to your previous contacts. Re-introduce yourself, explain you are looking for a job change and see if they can help get your CV into the right hands there.

Don't be shy about using all the contacts you have built up over the years to find out about new opportunities

Other good job sources are the national newspapers. Some of their website addresses are given below. There are too many regional newspapers to list here, but you can look in your own local newspapers for their web addresses.

www.telegraph.co.uk
www.thesundaytimes.co.uk
www.thetimes.co.uk
www.ijobs.independent.co.uk

www.observer.guardian.co.uk
http://jobs.guardian.co.uk
http://jobs.thesun.co.uk
http://jobs.dailymail.co.uk

Summary

There are so many good ways to identify employment opportunities and address them. There can be many pitfalls with the internet and you need to be on your guard. However, we believe that the potential positive outcomes outnumber the negative ones.

Business registers and directories can help you identify potential employers in your locale and, even for firms you have heard of, the directories can provide much helpful information about them to gather research data in order to better impress at interviews. Use this information to show the employer that you have done your homework about them and know better what you could be getting into. This shows tenacity, resourcefulness and intelligence.

The internet is expanding all the time and new websites keep cropping up, but the ones provided in this chapter should keep you going in the meantime!

SUNDAY
MONDAY
TUESDAY
WEDNESDAY
THURSDAY
FRIDAY
SATURDAY

Fact-check (answers at the back)

1. What job seeking approach do you think is more effective?
   a) Only going to the local job centre ☐
   b) Only looking at national or local papers ☐
   c) Asking friends and relations ☐
   d) Using as many routes as possible ☐

2. What is a good source of finding more inside information about suitable businesses and companies?
   a) The town hall, newspapers and magazines ☐
   b) Citizens Advice Bureaux, quangos and newspapers ☐
   c) Job centres, Citizens Advice Bureaux and Chambers of Commerce ☐
   d) National newspapers, trade magazines, business registers and directories ☐

3. From what main sources do most job vacancies come?
   a) The Civil Service and local authorities ☐
   b) Quangos, charities and the Civil Service ☐
   c) The public and private sectors, quangos and charities ☐
   d) The armed services, councils and the Civil Service ☐

4. Recruitment agencies:
   a) Should be avoided ☐
   b) Are a very useful route for job seekers ☐
   c) Are only used by unprofessional businesses ☐
   d) Are the only route you should use ☐

5. Which group of the UK public can use computer terminals free in libraries?
   a) Members with library cards ☐
   b) Any members of the public visiting the library ☐
   c) Members of the local authority ☐
   d) Just the librarians and their family members ☐

6. Where in the UK can you read all the daily newspapers free of charge?
   a) The doctor's surgery ☐
   b) The dentist's surgery ☐
   c) Most public libraries ☐
   d) The Town Hall ☐

7. How can you find out about local job and recruitment fairs?
   a) Local radio, television and your local newspapers ☐
   b) Your Member of Parliament ☐
   c) The Job Centre ☐
   d) Recruitment agencies ☐

8. What is the main purpose of business directories and registers?
a) To give you their addresses and phone numbers ❏
b) To show you their geographical distribution ❏
c) To explain what they do ❏
d) To provide data about companies' goods, services and financial status ❏

9. For which group is networking the most efficient source of employment?
a) The young and those leaving full-time education ❏
b) Older, experienced people who are looking for a job ❏
c) Married women with very young children ❏
d) The long-term unemployed ❏

10. When it comes to searching for a job, the internet:
a) Is useful in identifying recent vacancies and investigating more about a business or industry ❏
b) Is limited as not all jobs are advertised via the internet ❏
c) Will impress the business that you have computer skills ❏
d) Restricts you from contacting the company directly ❏

THURSDAY

Applying for advertised jobs

So far, we have prepared the ground meticulously having considered our predicament. We have put feelings of hurt and disappointment behind us, and have considered how to manage our limited financial resources and how we are going to move on. Our CV has been researched and written; we have examined our strengths and weaknesses, harnessing the former but remaining aware of the latter.

We have decided on the direction we want to go in and have embarked on a job search. We have considered the steps we plan to take to achieve our goal. Sources of fresh employment have been reviewed, we have prepared a plan and are now implementing it. Today we are going to apply for some of the jobs we have seen advertised and we are also going to do some prospecting to uncover other potential opportunities for replacing our prime source of income.

Applying for jobs in the public sector is different from the private, and we will also consider this. We will look at how to make the right impression in both scenarios and succeed in them. We will also take a brief look at Assessment Centres.

1 Applying for an advertised vacancy

When writing your covering letter, aim to keep it short – a maximum of two pages of typed A4 and ideally a single page. Lay out the letter neatly and try not to make it seem 'cluttered'. Keep to short paragraphs and, most of all, *keep it simple and to the point*. Always try to use good quality paper if submitting paper applications. The feel of a heavy paper in the hand provides a psychological impression of quality (of the sender).

All application letters should be typed, preferably on a computer. If it is absolutely not possible to type it, your writing must be neat and, again, layout is important. It is probably impossible to say as much in a single page of handwritten script as is possible in a typed one, so you may well have to run to at least two pages.

If job advertisements invite you to apply to a job title, for example, 'Write to the Personnel Manager describing how you fit the requirements of this post,' then telephone the organization first and ask for the Personnel Manager's first and surname. You can then start the letter 'Dear Ms Smith' or 'Dear Mr Smith' (if that is his or her name!) and finish it 'Yours sincerely,'.

Many advertisements are placed by recruitment consultancies, or only the name of the advertising organization and there is no indication of the location. In the case of a consultancy, you can telephone and ask the name of the consultant managing the assignment and then address your application letter to that individual personally.

However, if these approaches fail, you will have to address the letter to 'The Personnel or HR Manager', beginning it 'Dear Sir' or 'Dear Sir or Madam', and finishing it 'Yours faithfully,'. It is better to play safe and always begin the letter with the salutation 'Dear Sir or Madam'. At least that way you have covered all the possibilities and the personnel manager will definitely be male or female!

Some advertisers have titles such as 'Doctor' or 'Professor' or the like. Where that happens and you know the person's name, address the letter to 'Dr J Smith', begin it 'Dear Dr Smith' and finish it 'Yours sincerely,'. If it is not possible to obtain a name, begin the letter 'Dear Sir or Madam' and finish it 'Yours faithfully,'.

When signing letters, always ensure that your name is PRINTED underneath your signature. If you have a more formal title, such as 'Doctor', then by all means indicate this, but write in your first name as well so that the recipient of your letter knows your gender or, if unfamiliar with the first name, can make enquiries to ascertain gender if necessary.

This will save your respondent from appearing disrespectful in any reply or making some other gaffe when meeting you by mistakenly assuming you to be a man. This could cause needless embarrassment at a subsequent interview which might reflect adversely on you as a consequence.

Some advertisers invite you to 'Send replies addressed to Steve Smith'. It is better not to do so. Instead, address your letter to 'Mr S Smith', begin it 'Dear Mr Smith' and finish it with 'Yours sincerely,'. Never address your letter to 'Steve Smith' and then begin it 'Dear Steve Smith'. Even if Steve Smith does not know how to write a letter correctly, you can show that you do and he might be impressed as well.

The application letter should be neat, well spaced and contain short, succinct paragraphs and, ideally, no more than five or six. In the past we have received letters with corrections in them; with foreign substances such as jam, glue and Marmite adhering and, once, had one that had been all screwed up, smoothed out and sent anyway. This says a lot about the sender – none of it good!

Never pad out an application letter. It should be accompanied by an up-to-date CV and the letter should contain all the information requested, such as salary and anything else specifically asked for by the advertiser. Recruiters can receive hundreds of applications every day and they want to process them as quickly as possible. So make it easy for them. That way, your letter is more likely to receive a favourable response than one which is difficult to read, understand or is irrelevant.

Your supporting letter of application should be neat, concise and to the point – if it is to stand out from the crowd

Your covering letter should complement your CV and contain the information that your CV does not cover. Perhaps you have a standard CV that you use for all applications and you make the application specific through the content of the letter.

Alternatively, your CV may make passing reference to something which, for this application, needs emphasizing. In this case it is quite acceptable to repeat it or draw attention in your letter to that part of your CV which contains the appropriate text. For example, 'You can see from my CV that when I worked for Steve Smith & Partners, I had extensive experience in marketing and selling a similar type of widgets to those that you manufacture.'

It is important to sound knowledgeable and enthusiastic about the job and the organization. *'This is the type of position that I am seeking and, as your company is the market leader in this sector, I am ready for a greater challenge and particularly so to be working for the leading organization in its field.'*

Sometimes people apply for jobs and start from a negative position. Always **accentuate the positive** and seek ways of doing so. Instead of saying, '*Although I do not have any experience of working with widgets...,*' it might be possible to say something like, '*...During my time with Steve Smith & Partners, I had opportunities to see your widgets in action and very much want to be involved with such a dynamic and reliable product.*' This implies at least some knowledge of the product, enthusiasm for it and a commitment to it without actually saying much more.

Research on the organization is essential and is time very well spent. It increases your knowledge of the industry or market sector generally; helps to make you aware of who the key players are and, sometimes, can get you the job when you have very little sector experience to offer.

We know someone, who we will call Bob, who saw an HR job in furniture retailing in a multiple furniture department store group. However, Bob had very little retail sector experience but he applied for the job anyway. He was invited for an interview in a month's time. He phoned the company and asked for a list of all their branches. Bob went to the nearest ten armed with a camera and wrote a report on what he found. He presented it at his interview and got the job.

The object of the letter is to get you an interview. Make yourself sound interesting, intelligent, flexible, a team player, and above all, enthusiastic about working for the organization. Look at the advertisement, underline those requirements in applicants which you can meet and emphasize how you have done so in the past, how you have added value and give examples as well as describing specific and appropriate achievements.

If you know anyone who works for the company, phone them up and see if they can put in a word for you. Even if that is not possible, they may be able to give you some background information. You must be ready to use every weapon in your arsenal to achieve your objectives. Although you need to show yourself in the best light, *never ever tell lies*. You may be found out and, when you are, all is lost with that application.

Example of an application letter

Mrs G Evans
Human Resources Manager
ABC Pharmaceuticals
3 Princes Square
Slough
Berkshire
SL31 2BX

Spring Cottage
12 Orchard Avenue
Maidenhead
Berkshire
SL45 9AE
22 June 2012

Dear Mrs Evans,

Sales Administrator – Maidenhead Chronicle 20 June 2012

I am writing to apply for the above position and enclose my CV. You will see that I have been in sales administration in various roles for the last 15 years.

Recently I was one of a significant number of people whose jobs became redundant at Flash Bang Wallop & Co Ltd in Slough. Although this came as a shock, I have realized it has also provided an opportunity. Yours is a local company I have much admired over the years and I know a couple of people who work for you and they say ABC is a very progressive company and a happy place to work.

At Flash Bang Wallop, I was in the Sales department for ten years and produced statistical reports showing global monthly sales figures by category for every region and the country in which our fireworks were sold. In addition, I compiled stock figures from all the retail outlets in Europe which we supplied and passed these to the regional sales managers and their merchandisers. I am skilled in Excel, Access & SAP, speak French and German and also prepared sales turnover figures to other departments in the company including Finance.

I was Employee of the Month three times in the last five years and received a free weekend with my husband in a hotel each time. It has been wonderful working for Flash Bang Wallop and I am very sad it has ceased trading. My hobbies include keeping fit and I have twice run in the London Marathon.

Please invite me for an interview. We have so much to offer each other.

Yours sincerely
Janice Scott (Mrs)

2 Prospecting letters

If you know the sort of job you want to do, you may know the sort of organizations that employ people in your type of occupation. Before thinking about writing a prospecting letter to them, it is always a good idea to do some research first. Go to your public library and ask for the section where the business registers and directories are kept. From these sources you can usually obtain the names of companies, their addresses, locations, telephone numbers, a list of directors, numbers of people employed, gross annual turnover, the names and locations of subsidiaries and associated companies, as well as details of trade names, main product categories, websites and email information.

Write down or print out all the information that you think is relevant. The size of the organization can indicate opportunities. If the chairman or managing director is well known, make a note of that. Some of these people have honorary or aristocratic titles such as 'Sir Steven Richards'. Your letter should be appropriately addressed and should begin, 'Dear Sir Steven,' and finish 'Yours sincerely,'. It could also begin 'Dear Sir,' and finish 'Yours faithfully,'. Letters after names can indicate degrees, professional status and decorations and these should always be included. Make a note of them, the order in which they appear and always ensure you use them correctly.

Keep an eye on the business newspapers too (e,g, *Financial Times, The Times, Guardian, Observer, Daily Telegraph* and *The Sunday Times*). They often contain articles about companies which you can then research and approach direct, even quoting the article as well, to show your interest and commitment. All research you unearth is potentially valuable to you. It can be used in your prospecting letter, at an interview if you get one, and subsequently if you join the organization.

There is a section in most commercial directories which details types of company (e.g. marketing or engineering concerns). You can make a list of companies to look up in the reference section when you are seeking names, addresses and locations. It can often be useful to know the name of the company's chief executive, other directors and senior managers, so that your prospecting letter can be appropriately addressed to one of them. It has a much greater chance of getting to the right desk if it is addressed to a named person.

The chief executive of a large corporate concern is unlikely to respond to you personally, but may well pass the letter to the appropriate manager to do so on his/her behalf. This does therefore provide at least some chance that your letter may be seen by the most senior person in the organization and, who knows, in some cases it may strike a chord and have the desired result. In any case, any manager receiving a request from the chief executive to reply to a letter will be sure to do so.

For prospecting letters, use many of the appropriate tips given in Section 1 above. In some ways, a 'cold canvass' letter is easier to write than one where you are applying for a specific vacancy because you can stress all the strengths you have without having to compromise what you want to say to conform with narrow job and candidate specifications.

If you are applying to an organization which has European or international operations, and you have an appropriate language qualification, stress it. If you have more than one language, mention them all, together with levels of proficiency.

When phrasing a prospecting letter, you could use the following example as a guide, or something of your own along similar lines. One of the most important things about prospecting letters and covering letters is that they should be free of spelling and grammatical errors. Many managers and those in HR see such errors in a very negative way. In some cases, errors can have humorous repercussions such as the real ones below:

- *'I am a perfectionist and rarely if if ever forget details.'*
- *'Instrumental in ruining the entire operation of XYZ chain store.'*
- *'Reason for leaving my last job was maturity leave.'*

3 Application forms

Personally, we believe that application forms actively prevent applicants from demonstrating originality of thought, creativity

Example of a prospecting letter

Mr S Smith
Personnel Manager
ABC Pharmaceuticals
3 Princes Square
Leicester
LE3 2XJ

Spring Cottage
12 Orchard Avenue
Cambridge
CB3 2SZ
30 June 2012

Dear Mr Smith,

I was recently one of a significant number of people whose jobs became redundant to requirement at AJCS & Co Ltd in Cambridge. Although this came as a shock, I have realized that it has also provided an opportunity. Yours is a local company I have much admired over the years and I am enclosing a copy of my CV.

While my chief ambition is to continue in project management, I would be interested in discussing any vacancy you may have, or envisage having during the next 12 months or so, for which my knowledge, skills and experience may equip me. Any short-term temporary/freelance opportunity would be of interest in the interim too.

My particular strengths lie in *a, b, c and d* and I have added value during the last four years through leading a number of projects concerning *e, f, g and h*. These led to the following results which my team achieved on time and within budget: *j, k, l and m*.

If you have nothing for which I might be suitable now but know of any opportunities elsewhere within our sector, I would be grateful for any advice and guidance you can offer me in this respect.

Thank you so much for taking the time to read my letter and CV.

Yours sincerely
Janice Scott (Mrs)

N.B. The italicized letters above (*a, b, c and d; e, f, g and h; j, k, l and m*) refer to specified but unnamed strengths, project titles and team results. Replace these letters with your own information.

in presentation and any opportunity to provide an adequate explanation of any personal situation which deviates from the perceived norm. Nevertheless, these things have to be completed if you are going to get off the starting blocks.

If possible, photocopy or scan the blank form first. If this is impossible, make notes of what you need/want to enter into the various sections of the form. If you have a PC and a scanner, this makes things a lot easier because you can practise what you want to express. You can also reduce the point size to fit as well and can cut and paste from your CV or other relevant documentation.

All this is hugely frustrating and, even more so, if you have to complete more than one form a day. However, you can compensate for the restricting nature of application forms to some extent by enclosing your CV but some organizations actually forbid you from doing that as well!

Completing the form

Read it through from beginning to end before you do anything.
This prevents you from putting something in an earlier box which comes up again later but requiring more detail or a different interpretation from the one you had understood. Also, headings on standard forms are frequently ambiguous and the real sense of what they seek may not begin to become clear until you have read everything. Sometimes the form is accompanied by instructions on how to complete it (e.g. in black/blue ink only; in capitals; leaving no spaces etc), so you need to wade through all this stuff too.

There is often (with the more enlightened employers) a section calling for opinions, experience, special knowledge, skills, attitudes and experience (K, S, A & E) and sometimes another box for adding anything else (original thoughts, etc). Never fill these in without some thought and planning first.

Write notes for every section on a piece of paper or type them up. Consider these for relevance. If you want to express more than the form space allows, try to condense your words to fit but without diluting essential information or the sense you wish to impart. Be careful not to make mistakes when trying to squeeze text in to limited space. Cutting and pasting text from your CV is particularly useful when entering your personal details, qualifications and employment history.

Anything you cannot get on the form can be put in the letter which accompanies it or you could attach an extra sheet of your own containing a reference to the section it is supporting.

Try to think of the form as an extension of your own CV. If you are not allowed to send a CV with the form, you can use your CV as the basis for the information you enter on the form. This will also confirm consistency if, at some later stage in the selection process, you **are** permitted to provide a CV.

If you reach the end of the form with nothing else to add but there is a box enabling you to do so, go back over the form and read again those sections you had to condense for lack of space. You can then refer back, using your comments sheet, to the previous heading(s) and add the thoughts you would have expressed earlier had the inflexibility of the form not prevented you from doing so!

Consider too how you can emphasize (or re-emphasize) your strengths relevant to the post advertised and list them in relation to the stated requirements of the job. If you have had previous experience and/or knowledge of this, then bring these out too and write them as persuasively as you can.

Try to use the dynamic action verbs listed in the CV section. Practise writing these on your comments sheet to ensure it will fit into the space on the form if you are doing it in hard copy. When you are completing the form online, try to download it onto a CD or your hard drive.

Sometimes, the software used by the advertiser can be incompatible with your own IT set-up. Do not be afraid to phone the employer and ask for the form to be supplied in a format you **can** use: Adobe Acrobat or Word for example.

When you receive a form that you are not going to complete immediately, store it in a book or something else which will keep it flat, clean and ready for use.

Always return the form with a covering letter which re-emphasizes briefly the relevance of your knowledge, skills, aptitudes and experience (K, S, A & E) to the job and also remember to enclose a CV unless they have prohibited it.

Assessment Centres

If subsequently you are invited for an interview you need to be extra wary. In public sector organizations, interviews are almost always carried out by a panel of interviewers sitting together and sometimes there is an Assessment Centre beforehand at which you compete with other applicants. These encounters can last from a couple of hours to a whole week, with unsuccessful applicants dropping out voluntarily or compulsorily along the way until only two or three survivors remain. They can be fun or intimidating depending on your own outlook.

Managing job applications

Some sort of basic administrative system to manage all the applications you are making is needed. For some, you may need different versions of your CV and also a copy of your application letter, the job details (if you responded to an advertisement) and any notes you have made concerning the organizations you are dealing with. It can be embarrassing if you go for an interview only to discover the company has a different version of your CV than the one you have taken with you. The table below is an example of how to keep track of job applications.

Employment search control sheet

Employer details	Source	Date app. sent	Enclosures sent	Interview date(s)	Result Y/N

You will also need to keep hard copies of everything you have sent to employers so that, should you be invited for an interview, you will be able to take with you copies of the same documents they have. It is also a good idea to take extra copies of your CV in case the employer wants more copies. Always try to have six CVs with you wherever you go and also business cards.

Try to keep your control sheet up to date. If employers do not respond within a couple of weeks, phone them to check they have received everything. It is a sad reflection of the times we live in that many employers will not even acknowledge receiving your CV and enclosures let alone send a proper reply.

Maintaining motivation in spite of setbacks

'Success is moving from failure to failure without any loss of enthusiasm.'

Sir Winston Churchill

This quote from Sir Winston Churchill is not just his normal wit; it refers to the fact that during the early stages of World War II, Britain was constantly losing battle after battle. In the same way, you might apply for job after job and not initially succeed. Maintaining motivation is all to do with expectations and it is to these which we will turn now.

Too low expectations

Put very simply, if you do not expect to get a job, or do not expect to be successful in the interview, then this can become a self-fulfilling prophecy. In addition, having too low expectations can lead to depression about your present situation and result in lack of motivation and energy to seek work and market yourself.

Another disadvantage of having too low expectations is that you may start applying for jobs that are not challenging and end up in a job that is beneath your aptitudes and abilities and you may find yourself on the job market once again.

Try to maintain realistic expectations about your chances at getting a job – if you lose belief in yourself you will be at a disadvantage before you've even started

Too high expectations

In this case you may believe you can get a new job quickly or you may start applying for jobs that are too senior or too demanding. When it comes to seeing an advertisement, you might apply for the job and expect to be interviewed the following week. Having too high expectations means having more rejections and needing to wait for decisions longer than you anticipated.

As the selection process is not very exact or scientific you could end up being selected for a job that is unsuitable. Basically, you will have been selected for a job that represents your level of incompetence and you will soon be on the job market again.

Realistic expectations

Look at all your strengths, your past achievements and balance them out with your weaknesses and arrive at an image of yourself. Discuss your strengths and weaknesses with work colleagues, look at past appraisals and the results of psychometric tests.

Once you have done this, then apply for jobs that may be stretching and challenging but still comprise work you know you can do. Those with realistic expectations know that it may take a few months before they start their next job. They know that they might not be successful in the majority of interviews despite sending off CVs for posts they are ideally suited to. Realistic people see each interview as a learning experience.

Summary

Letters of application and prospecting letters to companies you would like to work for should come across as well thought through and professional. Make them neat but succinct and see if you can address them to an individually named person – you might have to phone the company to find out who that is!

Some organizations have application forms and these can be rather restricting – so send your CV or resumé as well. Always read through the application form to find out precisely what they are looking for. Use the simple control sheet to keep track of all the jobs you are going for.

Take care and show you are conscientious and remember you are trying to get an interview. Do not expect instant success and remain motivated – do not be pessimistic or too optimistic, your aim is to be realistic.

SUNDAY
MONDAY
TUESDAY
WEDNESDAY
THURSDAY
FRIDAY
SATURDAY

Fact-check (answers at the back)

1. Letters of application:
a) Should tell the employer everything they need to know ❏
b) Should be succinct but indicate that you know something about the company already ❏
c) Are not important as the prospective employer only reads your CV ❏
d) Should be addressed 'to whom it may concern' ❏

2. Use words and expressions in letters of application:
a) That accentuate the positive ❏
b) That include your weaknesses ❏
c) That expand in detail why you want the job ❏
d) That reflect who you are but do not necessarily show you have a good command of grammar and syntax ❏

3. Prospecting letters:
a) Are sent out to those companies that have advertised jobs ❏
b) Should never be sent out ❏
c) Do not indicate that you know something about the business ❏
d) Are sent out to companies you would like to work for who aren't currently advertising a vacancy ❏

4. Application forms:
a) Do not restrict what you have to say about yourself ❏
b) Should be filled in immediately without reading through carefully first – it is what they want ❏
c) Can restrict what you say, so send your CV also ❏
d) Never bother with them ❏

5. When applying for jobs your attitude should be:
a) You will get an interview quickly ❏
b) Optimistic ❏
c) Assume you will be looking for your next job for many months ❏
d) Apply for the most suitable jobs but be realistic about getting them ❏

6. For all letters of application and application forms:
a) Keep a hard copy – your applications might differ ❏
b) Just keep one copy – they are all the same ❏
c) Don't keep a copy, as you can remember all the things you said about yourself ❏
d) You do not need to send a letter of application and a CV with an application form ❏

7. When considering words and expressions in letters and application forms:
a) Be modest ❏
b) Use dynamic, positive-sounding words ❏
c) Just keep to the facts ❏
d) Exaggerate your achievements ❏

8. Each interview should be seen by you as:
a) A test of acceptability ❏
b) A test of your employability ❏
c) A test of your ability to impress others ❏
d) A learning experience ❏

9. If you have not heard from the prospective employer:
a) Phone them up to find out the situation ❏
b) Do not phone them – it sounds pushy ❏
c) Complain about their lack of manners ❏
d) Decide not to work for them even if they ultimately offered you a job ❏

10. In order to get a realistic picture of yourself:
a) Do not discuss your strengths and weaknesses with friends and colleagues ❏
b) Only ask friends about their perception of you ❏
c) Discuss your strengths and weaknesses with friends and colleagues ❏
d) Keep your strengths and weaknesses to yourself ❏

FRIDAY

The interview

We have now come almost full circle as we have covered all the aspects needed in order to obtain a job interview. This is the final hurdle and probably the most demanding. We will now equip you with everything you need to know to get that job offer, starting off with motivation, as employers are looking for self-motivated employees. Then we will move into the interview itself, the final hurdle of getting the job.

> *'He was fired with enthusiasm because he wasn't fired with enthusiasm.'*

Motivation

Before we look at the interview itself we need to discuss the issue of *motivation*. Motivation is the key to getting a new job because your prospective new employer will be trying to find out what motivates you? Why do you want to leave your present job? What motivates you to seek employment in his or her company? What aspects of the job on offer will motivate and enthuse you?

Understanding what motivates you is important because *all employers are desperately seeking motivated employees*. Employers are inclined to give jobs to those people who are motivated by something intrinsic to the job itself rather than to outside factors such as holiday entitlement or pay or conditions etc. It is often these outside factors that cause dissatisfaction at work but do not actually motivate people once they are achieved. As we shall see below, the outside factors are called **hygiene** factors and those factors intrinsic to the job are called **motivators.**

At the beginning of this book we hinted at some of the reasons why people become dissatisfied at work, and why the psychological contract between employer and employee has broken down. It is important to distinguish between what motivated you to leave your last job and what motivates you to seek another job or even in some cases a new career. Research by Frederick Herzberg, in the late 1950s in the USA, showed that causes of dissatisfaction at work were different from the causes of satisfaction. To put it another way, the factors that de-motivate people in the work environment are not necessarily the same as those which motivate them.

Herzberg referred to the causes of job dissatisfaction as **hygiene** factors. He used this term to suggest that these factors need to be addressed before employees would be in a situation to be truly motivated and that they would be motivated by a different set of factors which he referred to as the **motivators.**

The hygiene factors (which cause dissatisfaction at work but do not really motivate people when they are present) include the following:

- Company policy and administration
- Supervision and the relationship with the supervisor

- Working conditions
- Relationship with peers or subordinates
- The relationship between personal life and working life
- Salary.

Before you attend a job interview, try to work out what your motivators are

The motivators

Herzberg identified motivators as the factors that enthuse employees to put that extra effort into their work. In your letter of application, CV, and in the interview, mention must be made of one or more of the following factors that motivate you at work. Remember your prospective employer is seeking a *motivated* individual who can *add value* to his or her organization.

The motivators are:

- Something inherent in the work itself
- Growth within the role
- Advancement
- Achievement
- Recognition and responsibility.

The significant thing about these motivators is that they are all intrinsic to the job itself, whereas the hygiene factors are external to the job. Hygiene factors are only short-term motivators.

Work itself

The prime motivator for most people is something about the work that is inherently of interest to them. Fortunately people find different things of interest and so there are very motivated individuals in a great variety of jobs. Some individuals like administration, working in an ordered way and completing tasks. Other individuals like variety and change and can cope with a disorganized environment. Some individuals feel motivated because they like dealing in figures, others because they are making things, and others like working with people.

Generally people seek out jobs that match their interests, aptitudes and abilities. Indeed the interviewers will be asking themselves, 'Will this individual be happy doing this type of work?'

If you are unclear in your own mind what your aptitudes, interests and abilities are then seek career counselling, or an occupational psychologist could give you a range of tests that measure your interests and aptitudes.

If you have psychometric test results that show you have an aptitude for a particular type of work then put these results in your CV and certainly mention them in the interview. Psychometric tests are seen as 'evidence' whereas what you say about yourself is seen as less reliable.

Employers are on the lookout for those people who love the job itself, who are happy being busy in their work. If you can supply any evidence that the job you are applying for 'is you' then supply that evidence. Being enthusiastic about the job itself in the interview will reinforce your application.

Advancement

If you are applying for a job that is a step up, or a promotion, people never question why you are leaving your present job. Seeking promotion is seen as normal, understandable and an indication that you are motivated to move on to more challenging work. Promotion is also linked to the other motivators such as Growth, Responsibility, Recognition and Achievement. Saying you wanted promotion because you wanted more money, more status, or more power would not go down well as these are hygiene factors not motivators.

It is important in the interview to come over in a positive way. If your present job has become boring, do not mention this negative feeling but say you are seeking a 'fresh challenge' in your new job or that you 'now feel you have more to offer'. The interviewer might ask, 'Are you bored in your present job?' Your reply should be positive: 'The job on offer here sounds more interesting and challenging but I would not say I was bored with my present job.' This may, of course, be a little white lie but it is better than saying you were bored, a term that smacks of idleness and dissatisfaction. Employers do not want to employ dissatisfied individuals!

Growth

Growth is about new experiences, new responsibilities, acquiring new skills and learning new things. Growth is an important motivator and it also implies that you are flexible. In this era of change flexibility is increasingly seen as an important attribute. If you do not have some of the skills required in the new job then show enthusiasm to learn those new skills and point out that you have the attributes to learn those skills quickly.

Achievement

Your CV should have indicated your recent achievements and how you have added value to your most recent employer. For many of us we take our achievements for granted as they are an inherent part of the job. Even if you were part of a team that was responsible for a project or developed a new system or process, these are still achievements to be proud of.

A sense of achievement can be gained through continuous improvement, ideas that you have been responsible for or some aspect of the management of change. Look at the job on offer and imagine what sense of achievement you would gain from it. For teachers it is the growth and development and educational successes of their pupils. For the architect it is the building they helped to design; for the secretary or production worker it is the quality of the work they produce and so on.

Designing things, reaching targets, discovering things, changing things and dealing with customers can all give us a sense of achievement.

Recognition

Another great motivator is getting recognition for your achievements, or even recognition for a job well done. You should not be too modest when you are applying for a new job; sell yourself with your CV and sell yourself in the interview. If you have received recognition in your previous job then mention it.

Do not forget the indirect forms of recognition that you might have received such as a bonus, new responsibilities and promotion. If you were salesperson of the year then mention it in the interview. You can say it in a manner that does not sound like bragging, for example, 'I really enjoyed that job and became salesman of the year' or 'I enjoyed looking for better ways to do things so much that I was promoted to an internal consultant's role.'

Responsibility

Employers are looking for those staff who will take on responsibility and ownership for things. Responsibility is a motivator that goes with growth, recognition and achievement. Indicate that you seek responsibility, that you want to use your initiative, that you want to make your own decisions and that you want to manage yourself.

There is nothing an employer likes to hear more than an employee who says, 'Leave it with me', or takes ownership for things and uses their own initiative. The majority of people enjoy, and gain satisfaction from, taking on responsibility.

The interview

You have now identified the key motivators in your last job and the job for which you are applying. You have successfully marketed yourself and you have an effective CV, the next stage is the inevitable interview. The key things to remember when the letter arrives asking you to the interview are set out below.

1 Preparation and research

Ideally, you should have done this before you sent off your CV, but if you have not, then do so before the interview. It always impresses employers when applicants have bothered to research data about their organization. There is nothing so impressive as saying, *'It seems your company is expanding in such and such a field. I might well be of value to you in that area as I have considerable experience in...'* or *'Would my fluent French be of value to you as I see you are expanding in France?'* or *'I see that you are introducing self-managed teams and "lean" manufacturing techniques. I have some/considerable experience in these areas.'*

2 Revise your relevant strengths

Look at the job description and **compare your strengths with what is expected of you.** This gives you an opportunity to sell yourself on your strengths during the interview. If you lack experience in specific areas, then prepare answers to difficult questions in these respects. Try to anticipate the sort of questions you are likely to be asked.

What are your weakest areas in relation to the job? How can you counter probing questions in these areas? Emphasize your willingness to be trained or even offer to take a lesser job in which to gain more knowledge and experience first.

Before you go to the interview, think of ways you can add value to your new employer. A good method is to think of the ways you have added value, or could have added value,

SUNDAY

MONDAY

TUESDAY

WEDNESDAY

THURSDAY

FRIDAY

SATURDAY

to your last employer and remember the terms 'continuous improvement' and 'management of change'.

Employers are looking for self-motivated individuals who are clear about where their strengths lie and the direction they want to move in

3 Prepare to answer specific questions

Looking at your CV and the job description, you can envisage the type of questions you might be asked and be prepared to answer them. There are plenty of predictable questions which interviewers seem to ask, such as:

● Where do you see yourself in five years' time?
● What did you like most/least about your present/last job?
● What attracted you to this job?
● What other jobs have you applied for and why?
● You only stayed in your most recent company for two years, why was that?

4 Double-check the date, time, (likely) duration and location of the interview

It is no good preparing to give the best interview of your life, if you do not arrive at the right place at the appointed time. It is better to arrive half an hour early than one minute late for the interview and it gives you a chance to sit in Reception reading through information about the company and the products and services that it supplies.

Locate exactly where the interview is and then go and find somewhere quiet nearby to go through your papers. Make sure you have taken with you a copy of the advertisement of the job, or details about it if you heard of it through some other source. Also take a copy of your application letter, a copy of the application form (if you were required to complete one) and spare copies of your CV.

Try to think yourself into the job and ensure you can recall why you applied for it, the key facets of your appropriate knowledge, skills and experience. Consider too the sort of difficult questions which may be posed and practise answers in your mind. Think as well of any matters you want to be explained.

Being interviewed

First impressions

Research has shown that however objective interviewers try to be, they end up with 'impressions' of the candidate when they first meet them. These first impressions tend to stay with the interviewer so it is important that the *interviewee creates a good or acceptable impression early on in the interview.*

One of the most obvious ways to create a good impression is to dress in an appropriate manner. **Dress** ought not to be important but it is perceived by the prospective employer as an indication of the seriousness the interviewee takes the interview process. It also says something about personal standards of social awareness and behaviour.

The second method of creating a good impression is **to look and sound enthusiastic** and do not forget to **smile**. Conveying the impression of enthusiasm, humour and energy goes a long way to securing a job. It is also indicative of confidence to **shake hands** with the interviewer. This is not really possible if you have a panel interview where there are more than four people.

First impressions at the interview are crucial – make sure yours are good

Body language

Being too conscious of your body language could make you nervous so it is a good idea to just list a few do and don'ts.

DO

- Look relaxed with an open body posture.
- Maintain eye contact with the interviewer(s).
- Smile when you answer questions.
- Look interested in the questions.
- Give confident, enthusiastic replies.
- Use head and hand movements to add emphasis to your replies.
- Remember that a palms-up hand gesture indicates honesty or uncertainty, whilst palms down indicate certainty or a factual statement.
- Mirror the posture or gestures of the interviewer. Better still use similar gestures and postures but ones which are not exactly the same.

DO NOT

- Fold arms or cross legs, it looks defensive.
- Shift about in your seat when asked difficult questions. This is where the word *'shifty'* comes from and indicates stress or dishonesty.

- Look away or down. Lack of eye contact indicates poor confidence or evasiveness.
- Sit in a rigid or unmoving way. This indicates coldness.
- Mumble or sigh as this can be seen as covering-up something.
- Sit slumped in the chair. Can be perceived as not caring or even as insulting those interviewing you.
- Sit too close to the interviewer, as this is perceived as invading their personal space.
- Point your finger, even in jest. You can be animated but finger pointing, or battoning, is seen as rude and aggressive.

Establishing rapport

Your aim in the interview is to establish a good relationship with the interviewer(s) and one method for establishing this rapport is to get on to the same 'wavelength' as them. The way to do this is not only to adopt the most appropriate body language but also to *adopt the same mode of thinking as the interviewer.*

Generally speaking people tend to think in three different ways – some are *visual* thinkers, some are *auditory* thinkers and some are *kinaesthetic* thinkers. To put it more simply, visual thinkers usually think in terms of pictures; auditory thinkers tend to think in terms of sounds and kinaesthetic thinkers think in terms of feelings, touch and texture.

We can find out the type of thinker the person is by the words they use. Visual thinkers will tend to use words like: *see, picture, vision, bright, dull, clarify, illustrate, focus* and so on. Auditory thinkers use words like: *sound, accent, amplify, discuss, listen, loud, voice* and *say*. Kinaesthetic thinkers use words like: *active, warm, hold, sensitive, move, grab, touched* and *feel*.

The way to establish rapport with your interviewer is to **use the same types of words** when replying to their questions. If they ask you about your *vision* for the team's future you might reply that you *see* a good outcome and that both you and the team are *clear* and *focused*. What you are doing here is feeding back visual words with which the interviewer is comfortable.

It does not help to establish rapport if you feed back different words that may make the interviewer feel less comfortable. For example, they might ask, 'How do you *feel* about the future?' and you reply, 'The future *looks* **bright**.' The better reply to that question would be, 'The team and I are *sensitive* about the issues coming up in the next few months and are *actively* moving forward.' In this case you are replying to kinaesthetic words with more kinaesthetic words. Fortunately for most of us, we tend to subconsciously adopt the same types of words as those we talk to, so we do not have to think about it most of the time.

Answering questions

Technical and professional competencies

Selection for interview indicates that the interviewers have decided that you have the appropriate technical or professional competencies for the job but they will probably want to check your experience and its relevance to the new job. Most of the questions you can answer from your past experience and skills. Some of the skills and competencies you have acquired over the years have become second nature to you now and there is a danger that you will fail to sell your skills in an appropriate manner.

It is a good idea to use expressions like 'very experienced', 'conversant' or 'fully competent' in replying to some of the technical questions. If you are asked about technical or professional skills which you do not have, then you can still reply in a positive manner: '*I am enthusiastic about learning those additional skills*' or '*My aptitude and existing skills in that area will ensure I can learn those new techniques very quickly and apply them competently.*'

Intra-personal and team competencies

There can be a danger that interviewers may concentrate on your technical competencies when in fact they should spend at least half the interview checking out your 'team and intra-personal skills'. (Note, intra-personal is how you manage yourself and team is how you relate to others.) An engineer talking to another engineer about engineering does not give the interviewer a rounded picture of the candidate and it may ignore some of the interviewee's major strengths (or weaknesses).

If the interviewer is concentrating on the technical and professional area, an *astute interviewee can give answers that include their other strengths*. A way of introducing the additional strengths would be to answer questions in the following way: 'I am *very experienced in using that software* (technical competence) indeed *I led the team* that introduced it into the company and *I coached others* in its use (team competence), 'or'I have *three years experience in selling* pharmaceutical products (professional competencies) and I *train* and *coach* new sales staff and *chair team meetings* (intra-personal and team competencies)'. The importance of intra-personal and team competencies cannot be over-estimated. It is these competencies that will ultimately show whether the individual fits in with the company culture and whether or not they will succeed as managers and/or team leaders.

Intra-personal and team competencies include the following: constructively working with others; coaching and giving feedback; communication, customer relations, meeting skills, mentoring, counselling, leadership and so on.

Many jobs these days require people to be 'team players' and in the interview the interviewee should stress their team working experience. Enjoying team working, being an 'accepted member' of the team, having effective people skills and customer care skills are good terms to use.

Jobs which involve managing others require listening skills, questioning skills, appraisal abilities, facilitating, giving feedback, motivating others, leadership, administrative skills and awareness of team dynamics and the way emphasis fluctuates between the needs of the business, the team and the individuals within it.

Questions with an emphasis on behaviour

Modern interviewing techniques stress that questions should be about the interviewee's **behaviour** not about some hypothetical situation. A behavioural question would be: *'In your* *present job I'm sure you have come across difficult or awkward customers. Give us an example of a difficult customer you have come across recently and how you dealt with them?'* Having given a reply to this question, a common follow-up question would be: *'What did you learn from that experience?'* or *'Would you behave differently today after thinking about the situation?'*

Some interviewers may ask hypothetical questions such as: *'What would you do if you had to deal with a difficult employee or difficult customer?'* These questions tend to lead interviewees into giving textbook type answers and not the real behaviour of the interviewee. The astute interviewee can turn these questions round to give a more personal and 'real' answer. A more effective response would be: *'I inherited a difficult employee in my last job* (real event) *and I tackled them in the following way* (real behaviour)...'

Typical interview questions

In many ways you can predict the type of question that interviewers might ask during the interview.

Opening questions

These are designed to establish rapport and make both parties feel at ease. *'How did you get here today?'* or *'Why did you decide to take a degree in Bio-chemistry?'* are broad questions that break the ice and get the conversation to flow.

Another opening question may be *'What do you know about our company?'* This question hides two other questions, *'Have you done your homework for this job'* and *'How seriously are you taking this interview and job?'*

Some opening questions can be a bit more demanding:

- *Why do you want to leave your present job?*
- *Why were you selected for redundancy?*
- *What other jobs are you applying for and with what sort of organizations?*
- *Are you just restricting your search to the local area where you live?*
- *What has attracted you particularly to this job or our company?*

Professional and technical competencies

Needless to say, questions will be asked to find out if you can do the job or not. The CV will have indicated that you have the qualifications or experience but these have to be checked in the interview. Typical questions are:

- *Are you familiar with XYZ software?*
- *What research/technology are you working on at the moment?*
- *You said in your CV that you spent a lot of your time on monoclonal antibodies (or blue tooth technology or competence development etc), please expand on this for me.*
- *You say you are responsible for Project Management. What are the key stages of a project in your own mind?*
- *Name four essential skills required in your current job?*
- *In your present job you sell widgets, but we produce grommets. Do you think your style of selling will need to change?*
- *You claim that you increased productivity in your department by 15 per cent. How would you go about increasing our productivity?*
- *Are you responsible for the budget in your department? If so, tell us about the current issues.*
- *Tell me about some of the technical/work problems you have faced during the last year and how have you solved them?*
- *How do you see the profession developing over the next five years?*
- *From your experience, what attributes does a good manager/ leader have?*
- *How have you added value to your department/organization over the past two years?*
- *We have a dozen other candidates, so what can you offer us that makes you stand out as special?*
- *How do you see your long-term career developing over the next five years?*

Systems and procedures

All companies have different systems and procedures, so it is unlikely that you would be asked questions in this area. The exceptions are for those people who are going for jobs where they have to design or enforce systems and procedures. Such jobs are in Health and Safety and Human Resource Management.

In such cases the systems and procedural questions are really professional and technical questions.

Intra-personal and team competencies

It is very possible that the other candidates have the same professional and technical qualifications as you do, otherwise they would not have been selected for interview. In this case you are more likely to get the job on your intra-personal and team skills.

- *As a team leader, how would you describe an effective team?*
- *What are your strengths and weaknesses when it comes to managing people?*
- *How did you overcome the employees' resistance to the changes you introduced?*
- *Describe a difficult customer/employee you have encountered over the last couple of years and how did you handle them?*
- *You say in your CV that you are a team player; please describe a situation where these skills have been evident?*
- *What vision do you have for your present team over the next year?*
- *How have you persuaded your team to accept the vision and strategy?*
- *Give us an example of where your leadership failed (or you feel you could have done better) and what did you learn from that experience?*

Types of question

Open

These are the most common questions in an interview. The question is open in the sense that it encourages longer answers. Often the question starts with *How* or *Why* or *In what way* and is designed for the interviewee to talk about their experiences and achievements. Other open questions begin with *Where*, *When* and *Who*.

Closed

The closed question is one where a single word or short sentence could constitute an answer. '*How many years have you*

worked for the company?' or 'Can you drive?' are examples of
closed questions. Most interviewers do not ask closed questions
unless they want commitment or seek to identify a lack of it.

When asked a closed question, the astute interviewee will
give a much more elaborate answer than initially the question
seems to warrant. The single-word answer such as 'yes' or 'no'
should be avoided and more information about successes and
achievements could be introduced into the answer.

Hypothetical

Hypothetical questions are designed to find out how you would
behave under certain circumstances or what your attitudes
are. They usually start off with the expression: 'What would
you do if...?' or 'Imagine you are in XYZ situation, how would
you cope?' Hypothetical questions tend not to be very useful
because they lead to hypothetical answers that may not
reflect a person's real behaviour. If you are asked hypothetical
questions then the best approach is to answer them from your
own experience or behaviour, e.g. 'A similar thing happened to
me last year and my approach then was to...'.

Leading

Leading questions are those where the correct answer is
obvious such as 'This job involves a lot of driving. Do you like
driving?'. If you are asked a leading question, the best approach
is to give expanded answers so that you have an opportunity to
sell your 'added value' skills.

Probing

Probing questions are those that explore for more information
and often come as a follow-up to other questions. Examples
include, 'So how did you feel about that?' or 'What was the outcome
of your decision?' or 'Would you do the same thing again?'

Behavioural

The behavioural question tries to find out your attitudes or
behaviour based on your **real experience** in work. A typical

question would be, *'You mentioned difficult customers. Give us an example of difficult customers you have come across in the past year and how you managed them.'* If you are asked a behavioural question it gives you an opportunity to bring in some of your skills and attributes.

Rephrasing negative questions

Some questions lead you into areas where you do not want to go, so the best approach is to re-frame the question so that the answer is more positive: *'So 20 per cent of your team were dissatisfied with the changes. How did you manage them?'* A re-framed answer would be: *'Indeed 80 per cent of the team were won round and we used their enthusiasm to bring round the others'.*

Some interviewers tend to give a negative twist to events as if they are interrogating you. Again, you can re-frame the question; *'So, after six months the project was a failure?'* Your reply intends to play down the negative side or negative implication: *'Although the customer did not accept the proposal, we gained a lot from the process and we are now much better equipped to deal with a similar situation.'*

The most common negative question in an interview is: *'Tell us about your weaknesses?'* Needless to say the last thing you want to do is talk about your weaknesses when you are trying to impress. There are three re-framed approaches:

● First, mention weaknesses that are really strengths. *'Some colleagues accuse me of being a workaholic'* or *'I can be too much of a perfectionist.'*
● The second approach is only to admit weaknesses that you are doing something about, e.g. *'I am new to computers, so I have enrolled on an evening class called "IT for those in business.'*
● Finally you can openly admit your weaknesses but make sure they have no bearing on the job you have applied for, e.g. *'I'm not too fond of heights.'* Needless to say, you are more likely to be seen as plausible if you mention those weaknesses that you are aware of and are doing something about.

Comments about your last employer

During the interview, your last job and most recent employer are bound to be discussed. As a general rule, it is unwise to be critical of your last employer, however bitter you might feel. Being too critical may give the interviewer the impression that you will also be ultra-critical of any new employer.

It can be useful to give the impression that you really enjoyed the work (professional and technical competencies) and thrived working with the team (interpersonal and team competencies). If you are critical of the last employer, then be critical in a constructive way, e.g. *'My job was no longer required as the company had made a strategic decision to move out of that line of business and was in the process of downsizing. I thought it was the wrong decision as I am certain that there is more business to be had in that sector.'*

Interviewers

The highly structured interviewer

The highly structured interviewer tends to structure the interview very well and asks each candidate the same set of questions, so they can compare. The difficulty with this type of interviewer is that they have their agenda and they may not ask you those vital questions that allow you to talk fully about your strengths.

The skill is to bring in relevant skills and achievements during the interview as additional information. If you feel that a vital area has been left out then, at the end of the interview, you can comment that one of your areas of achievement has yet to be discussed and you can then prolong the discussion which suits your agenda.

The unstructured or disorganized interviewer

The disadvantage of such an interviewer is that they cannot really compare candidates. The advantage is that you can take over in a subtle way and talk about your skills and achievements. To a large extent the interview follows your agenda and you can give expanded answers to their questions. In addition you can even give information based on questions they have not actually asked you.

The aggressive interviewer

However rude and aggressive the interviewer, you should always try to remain calm and not rise to the bait. You should ignore their aggressive intonations and answer the basic points of the question. You can also rephrase the question so that a more positive slant can be given.

Panel interviews

Panels of three or more interviewers can be disconcerting, especially if different panel members have different agendas. Panel members tend to each ask one or two questions, then another panel member takes over. With small panels, such as three interviewers, they may ask a set of questions based round a specific subject area. As with all interviews, you should try to maintain eye contact with the person who is asking you the question but then give your answer to the whole panel.

Important note

It can happen at the end of the interview that the interviewer asks you whether, if selected, you would take the job. Your answer should always be in the affirmative. If you have any doubts about the job, you have plenty of time to accept the job or reject it between the actual interview and receiving and considering the offer letter.

Presenting yourself

How you come across during the interview is clearly very important. We have mentioned that you need to **smile** and **be enthusiastic** but you also need to come across as **confident** and **positive.** Moderation in all things is required here because you need to avoid being overconfident or seen as arrogant. The best approach is to mention your skills and strengths with practical examples of the positive outcomes.

To say you see yourself as *'an excellent team leader or a great motivator'* will not be as impressive as pointing out the results: *'I took over the de-motivated team and managed to re-direct them into raising production levels (productivity went up by 25 per cent) and, at the same time, team members became more enthusiastic. It was a challenge at the time but I turned them round.'*

The key to being positive and confident is to recognize that we tend to respond in four different ways to social situations. We can be *aggressive, passive, manipulative or assertive*. In the interview and work environment, we should show the skills of assertiveness and show confidence in ourselves. If, in the interview, you come across as aggressive, submissive or manipulative, you will not be offered the job.

Assertive expressions show self-confidence and include expressions like: *'I succeeded in...'; 'I persuaded senior management to...'; 'Productivity improved by 25 per cent after I introduced...'; 'My report led to a change in the strategy...';* One employee we interviewed said at the end of the interview, *'If you employ me I can assure you, you will not regret it'''* We did employ him and we did not regret it!

It is a characteristic of the British to be rather modest but this is not a trait to use in an interview. **Passive** expressions include: *'I might have had an impact....'; 'I think I can...'; 'I might have been responsible for...'; 'I kept a low profile...'; 'It wasn't up to me...'.* Expressions such as these convey a lack of confidence and are not the way to sell yourself in the interview.

In a similar way, coming across as **aggressive** in tone should also be avoided: *'The fools did not take my advice...'; 'You have got to be tough with such employees. I told them to shape up or ship out'; 'People do not matter when it comes to business decisions'; 'I left because senior management were incompetent'; 'I'm not noted for tolerating fools'; 'You can't get the staff these days. It's all dumbing down.'*

The inner dialogue

One of the best ways to come across as confident and relaxed is to **think yourself into being confident.** It is like method acting – if you think the part, you will be the part. You must try to convince yourself that you are one of the better candidates and that you have a lot to offer. To some extent it is giving yourself a good talking to, often referred to as the 'inner dialogue'.

Once you have convinced yourself that you are ideal for the job, your confidence will grow. Think of all the things at which you excel in the job; all the positive remarks about your performance which have been written in your annual appraisals. Read them again!

It is a cruel aspect of human nature that if you are desperate for the job, you will not come across very well but if you are relaxed about getting the job, you are more likely to be offered it. You should try to come across as enthusiastic but not desperate. Use the inner dialogue to improve your confidence but reduce stress by seeing the interview as an exercise and experience.

The end of the interview

At the end of the interview, you will probably be asked if you have any questions. You should have prepared one or two questions before the interview but they ought to be linked to the nature of the job itself, the people or team you are going to work with, career progression and training and development opportunities.

The time to talk about remuneration and fringe benefits is when you have received a written job offer and draft contract of employment. That is the point when the employer wants you and has proved it and is when you have maximum negotiating strength.

When you get up to leave, shake hands with the interviewer(s) and thank them for inviting you and you should reinforce your interest in the job: *'Thank you for inviting me along today. I am very interested in the position and the company itself sounds like the sort of place where I could fit in and do very well.'*

At the first opportunity after leaving, sit down and reflect on the interview while it is still fresh in your mind. What can you learn from this experience which might help you next time? Make brief notes of your thoughts.

Summary

Here we have described the whole interview process starting from the fact that the interviewers are looking for motivated individuals, and that research has shown that in the long term only six things motivate employees and that they are intrinsic to the work itself. Basically if you show you are more interested in the work itself than the pay and conditions you are more likely to be offered the job!

In the interview, think about the first impression you give and think of a few positive body language postures or gestures you could use. Tune into the mode of thinking of the interviewer(s). Remember that the interviewers are interested not just in your technical skills but how you work with others and how you manage yourself. Modern interviewers are also interested how you behave in your present job and will focus on your recent work experience and behaviour.

SUNDAY
MONDAY
TUESDAY
WEDNESDAY
THURSDAY
FRIDAY
SATURDAY

Fact-check (answers at the back)

1. Only one of the following is truly motivational:
   a) Pay/salary ❑
   b) Status at work ❑
   c) Working conditions ❑
   d) Responsibility ❑

2. Things that motivate us:
   a) Are extrinsic to the work we do ❑
   b) Are called hygiene factors ❑
   c) Are intrinsic to the work we do ❑
   d) Relate to how we are managed ❑

3. Which of the following is not considered motivational?
   a) Responsibility ❑
   b) Growth within the job ❑
   c) Achievement ❑
   d) Pay/salary ❑

4. Before you go for the interview:
   a) Think about how you have added value in your last job ❑
   b) Prepare to ask questions of the interviewer(s) about salary ❑
   c) Prepare to ask questions about holiday entitlement and sick pay ❑
   d) Think about the interview after this one – to calm you down ❑

5. Your body language in the interview:
   a) Is irrelevant ❑
   b) Should be something you are thinking about all the time ❑
   c) Will be ok if you just brush up on a few dos and don'ts ❑
   d) Can be ignored as first impressions are unimportant ❑

6. To establish rapport with the interviewer(s):
   a) Agree with all the things the interviewer says ❑
   b) Try to adopt the same mode of thinking as the interviewer(s) ❑
   c) Assume the interviewer thinks like you ❑
   d) Just talk about your strengths ❑

7. Intra-personal and team competencies refer to:
   a) Your technical skills ❑
   b) Competencies associated with systems and procedures ❑
   c) The way you manage yourself ❑
   d) The way you manage yourself and work with others ❑

8. The modern method of selection interviewing stresses:
a) Hypothetical questions ❏
b) Closed questions ❏
c) Behaviourally based questions ❏
d) Leading questions ❏

9. Negative questions should be:
a) Ignored ❏
b) Rephrased ❏
c) Shown to be negative ❏
d) Argued about ❏

10. In the interview you should come across as:
a) Assertive and confident ❏
b) Aggressive and confident ❏
c) Submissive and modest ❏
d) Manipulative and modest ❏

SATURDAY

Starting your own business

With all your experience and expertise you might decide to start your own business, to become self-employed. Both authors have worked for large organizations in both the public and private sectors and have also been self-employed. To be successful in self-employment you need to review your situation and your motivation. This is what we are going to look at now.

Preliminary planning

Think about what you want to do, whether there is a market for it and then consider your ability to provide what is required. Do you possess the knowledge and skills necessary to be successful? You are going to need many more skills than just those you have needed as an employee with a narrow job specification limited to just one main role.

For example, you may need manufacturing, warehousing and stores knowledge and experience (will your garage provide enough space and be sufficiently secure?). Can you directly sell your product(s) or service(s) or will you have to pay someone to do this and how much will it cost?

Are you going to buy a franchise, run somebody else's business as your own (e.g. as a pub tenant, sub-post office operative or similar) or set up something new of your own? The cost implications need to be considered.

If you plan to work from home, think about your own domestic circumstances.

Do you have children? What impact will this have on the business? Do you need to consider childcare provision etc. when you have to go away?

How will your spouse and/or other members of the family be affected? Are they going to be involved with the business and to what extent?

Will you be able to get your work done without interruptions to help with the washing up/have a chat with neighbours etc. when you need to be in your home 'office'?

Will your family understand that, when you are in your home 'office', you are not to be disturbed and that you are 'at work'?

Carry out a 'SWOT' analysis on yourself – **S**trengths. **W**eaknesses, **O**pportunities and **T**hreats. What are the outcomes from this exercise? (See Tuesday chapter.)

Do you have a hobby or an interest which could make money for you and form the cornerstone for a business enterprise? What special knowledge, skills, aptitudes and experience (K, S, A & E) do you have upon which you can capitalize in your business?

Do you have the support of family and friends as you go it alone?

Do you have a 'USP' (Unique Selling Point')? This could be a special skill or knowledge you could utilize, develop and exploit for a business purpose. How unique is your USP and what sort of an advantage will it give you over potential competitors?

What special K, S, A & E do you have which you can bring to your business to ensure it survives and prospers?

Secondary planning

Starting and running a business can be stimulating and very rewarding. It can also be exhausting, expensive, frustrating, and occupy an inordinately great amount of time with little to show for it at the end. It may be the single most significant step you take in your working life and you need to be sure that you are *really committed* to it and that you will see it through despite all obstacles which get in your way. You need to *plan* everything and leave nothing to chance.

Do you really possess the tenacity, dogged determination, persuasiveness and all the other qualities, knowledge, skills, aptitudes and experience for success?

You need to be the owner of the business, part-accountant and bookkeeper; marketing and sales executive; administration manager; IT specialist, customer service interface, stores and warehouse operative (if you are going to be dealing in goods). You are also going to be delivery operative (whether they be goods or services), business and people manager (if you are going to employ staff) and part-lawyer as well. These are a lot of hats to wear and you may need to wear them all some or much of the time.

Planning is the only logical way forward. You need to consider what your broad strategy is to be for the first one to three years and the specific aims and objectives you will need to put in place each year to meet your strategic intentions. A strategic business plan for three to five years backed up by an annual business plan are good starting points.

If you are going to need operating capital to start your business, you must consider from where this is going to come and, if your own resources are inadequate, who you can approach to provide the funding you will need and on what conditions. Often this is your bank manager. He or she will need to see your plans, both strategic and business as well as projected turnover, anticipated profit plan and cash flow forecast. Financial organizations providing fundings, such as banks, want their capital back and a healthy profit. After all, the bank is a business too.

Whatever the nature of your business, sound financial planning will be essential

Those responsible for taxation – in the UK it is HM Revenue & Customs (HMRC) – will need to know of your business intentions and, before you start trading, you need to register with HMRC and obtain a business reference number. If you plan to do work with local or central government departments, they will decline any involvement with you until you can produce your HMRC reference number. All those contacts have now moved online.

In the UK, if you have any general non-HMRC business queries, the Business Link network website can be accessed online at the following address: http://www.businesslink.gov.uk/mynewbusiness.

HMRC will also need to be informed before you start in case registration for VAT may be needed if your turnover is likely to exceed the minimum threshold in your first or early years. You may also need an accountant and you will definitely need a business bank account, 'books' for accounting or a bookkeeping system and printed stationery.

Basic office equipment is likely to include a computer, printer, possibly a scanner, a service provider and the means to connect to the internet. You may need a photocopier: a 3-in-1 system (black/white and colour copying, scanner and printer) is ideal. You will also need a landline telephone, probably a mobile phone and answering machine, a desk and chair, filing cabinet and dedicated work space. All of these cost money although much of the equipment can be acquired second hand.

You may also need a reliable car or van. IT support can be critical when working from home and you may need help urgently and unexpectedly. Money to live on and money to support the business must be considered as well. How much money will you need to live on and how much to support the business until regular income starts to flow? Most of all, how long can you live in the early stages with no money coming in?

Sensible budgeting is essential in advance. The table in the Sunday chapter would be a good starting point. You will also be responsible for paying your own National Insurance contributions and income tax, both paid now to HMRC but through different avenues.

Insurance is another subject to consider as you may need product, public and employer's liability insurance as well as professional indemnity insurance cover. The latter can be very expensive unless you belong to a professional body which has an overall umbrella professional indemnity policy for members who pay discounted premiums. This cover is essential if you are to be a Sole Trader or a Partnership.

Business status is important too. Will you be a Freelancer, a Sole Trader, a Partnership, a Limited Partnership or a Limited Company? You will probably need professional advice on this from a solicitor or accountant but some banks have starter kits explaining all this for new businesses plus free or subsidized banking services for an initial period.

Local business advisers (Business Link in the UK), can be a source of good, inexpensive and impartial advice and support. It may also run courses on setting up your business and, in the past, Business Links have provided some limited financial support in the first few months along with a helpline number for ongoing advice. Most Business Links also have a library of business reference publications which local small businesses can access.

When you are ready to start trading

Open a business bank account and try to keep business expenditure completely separate from personal and domestic transactions. Maintaining a personal bank account is useful and some people even have their business account with a completely different bank. This ensures that business transactions are unlikely to be confused with personal ones and vice versa.

Will you need planning permission? Generally, if you work from home and will not have business people visiting you there, on foot or by car, and your neighbours do not object, you probably will not have a problem. However, you should tell your mortgage provider and also check the terms of your lease or freehold document for any restrictions in this respect. Council tenants are not usually permitted to run a business from home.

You will need to tell the insurance company which covers your house and contents what you are doing (if you plan to work from home) together with the nature and value of the equipment you are using there. Usually this cover will be added to your basic domestic dwelling and contents policy as an endorsement and charged at a higher premium.

Your business image and credibility are important. It is worth investing in really good quality stationery and business cards as well as coming up with a suitable and impressive business name under which to trade. If you are going to have a logo, you will need to establish who owns it (especially if you get someone to design it for you) and it may be necessary to register it as a Trade Mark. This can be expensive and time consuming. You will also need invoices (although you can use your own headed paper for this), compliments slips and envelopes of different sizes and strengths depending upon what they will contain.

If you are going to set up as a Sole Trader, you may need to become a Limited Company later. It is a good idea to check with Companies House first to see if your planned name is already registered as a Company. If it is, you may need to choose a different name now and one that is not yet registered.

If the name is not registered, it may be worth protecting your name by registering it as a company name now but not actually trading until such time in the future when it will be appropriate. You will need to submit accounts to Companies House every year, even while not trading, but this costs just a nominal amount.

Consider how much you are going to charge for your services or products. In order to do so, you need to examine your planned sales volume and unit price(s), pricing variations and constraints. The selling price is what you will be charging for your goods or services and comprises your direct costs (the materials and services you buy in order to produce them) together with a mark-up to cover the cost of your overheads and profit.

You will need to research what your competitors are charging in order to be competitive yourself. If they are generally cheaper than you, ways will need to be found to reduce your overheads in order to compete or reduce your profit margin or have a USP or some other advantage that counter-balances the higher cost of your product(s) or service(s) in the marketplace.

Do you have what it takes?

Do you have what it takes to run your own business? In addition to any business skills you may need, your own personality and character are also very important. Successful entrepreneurs usually exhibit some or all of the following attributes. How do you measure up against them?

Initiative	Strong powers of persuasion
Flexibility	Independence
Creativity	Problem solving ability
Imagination	Will to win
Leadership	Perseverance
Moderate risk-taking	Conscientiousness
Belief in your own destiny	Ability to seek and take good advice
Tenacity	Literacy and numeracy
Practicality	Sense of humour

Go through the following 22 statements and rate yourself on a scale of 6, where 1 is very poor and 6 is outstanding. Circle the number which applies most appropriately. Remember, honesty is essential. If you cheat, you are only cheating yourself.

I can take advice	1	2	3	4	5	6
I get on with most people	1	2	3	4	5	6
I am enthusiastic	1	2	3	4	5	6
I can make considered decisions	1	2	3	4	5	6
I have specific aims and objectives	1	2	3	4	5	6
I am self-disciplined	1	2	3	4	5	6
I am aware of the risks	1	2	3	4	5	6
I have the support of my family	1	2	3	4	5	6
I will put in as much effort and work all the hours it takes	1	2	3	4	5	6

I can and do learn from my mistakes	1	2	3	4	5	6
I can cope with stress	1	2	3	4	5	6
I am in good health	1	2	3	4	5	6
I will not give up when the going gets tough	1	2	3	4	5	6
I have patience and know success may not be swift	1	2	3	4	5	6
I can motivate myself and others	1	2	3	4	5	6
I know when to relax and I do so	1	2	3	4	5	6
People often see my point of view	1	2	3	4	5	6
I am honest and possess integrity	1	2	3	4	5	6
I have a history of being an achiever	1	2	3	4	5	6
I really enjoy working on my own and coping	1	2	3	4	5	6
I have a keen sense of humour and can laugh at myself	1	2	3	4	5	6
I am resourceful	1	2	3	4	5	6
Total scores per column						
Grand total score:						

Add up all the numbers circled and record your score. If you have scored 105 or less, perhaps you should reconsider self-employment. Scores of 110–120 indicate that you probably have got what it takes, and those who score in excess of 125 are asked to contact us and tell us what your secret is! However, some quality assurance is advisable. Ask someone who knows you well to also complete this page about you. Add up the answers from both of them and divide the answer by 2. The outcome should be more reliable.

Summary

There is much more to starting a business than has been written here but this is the basic skeleton upon which the practice is built. Many of those who have chosen to be self-employed, and who still are after five years or more, will probably confirm that they get a lot of satisfaction from it. We certainly have and we have also made a good living from it. We have had some wonderful clients for whom we have been able to improve their businesses and help them to achieve higher quality standards in the management of their people. It is our sincere hope that this book will help you to find work that will fulfil you, give you much satisfaction and continue to provide your livelihood.

SUNDAY
MONDAY
TUESDAY
WEDNESDAY
THURSDAY
FRIDAY
SATURDAY

Fact-check (answers at the back)

1. Some acronyms have been used in this chapter. What does K, S, A & E stand for?
   a) Knowledge, Sensibility, Action and Education ☐
   b) Knowledge, Sensitivity, Attitude and Excellence ☐
   c) Knowledge, Skills, Aptitudes and Experience ☐
   d) Knowledge, Skills, Attitude and Education ☐

2. What are the best personal qualities you need to have for your own business?
   a) Tenacity, determination and persuasiveness ☐
   b) Toughness, determination and perseverance ☐
   c) Tenacity, diligence and personality ☐
   d) Thoughtfulness, decency and personality ☐

3. Where in the UK can you find a source of good, inexpensive and impartial business advice and support?
   a) In the public library ☐
   b) From the business press ☐
   c) The Citizens' Advice Bureau ☐
   d) From your local Business Link ☐

4. What data will the bank need in order to consider lending you money?
   a) Marketing plan, profit plan and business plan ☐
   b) Business bank account, professional liability policy and profit forecast ☐
   c) Projected turnover, anticipated profit plan and cash-flow forecast ☐
   d) Cash-flow projections, professional liability policy and marketing plan. ☐

5. Which business insurance policies will you need?
   a) Professional indemnity, office equipment and public liability ☐
   b) Employer's liability, product liability and office contents ☐
   c) Professional indemnity, employer's liability and public liability ☐
   d) Keyman Insurance, employer's liability and public indemnity ☐

6. What factors contribute to calculating the selling price of your goods or services?
   a) Direct costs + overheads + profit ☐
   b) Cost of materials + rent + insurances ☐
   c) Cost of transport + insurances + overheads ☐
   d) Overheads + insurances + travel ☐

7. If your competitors' goods are cheaper than yours how can you compete?
a) Have a better USP, lower overheads and offer inducements ❏
b) Reduce your profit margin, insurance premiums and offer incentives ❏
c) Stop being a Sole Trader and become a Limited Company ❏
d) Reduce your price as turnover is more important than profit ❏

8. If you plan to work from home, who should you tell and what should you check?
a) The police, your landlord/mortgage provider, and your home insurance policy ❏
b) Your landlord/mortgage provider, your home insurance company and check freehold documents ❏
c) The police, your neighbours and your home insurance company policy ❏
d) Your local council, the police and check your lease ❏

9. For what does the acronym SWOT stand?
a) Stationery, Work, Occupation and Tenacity ❏
b) Swiftness, Work, Opportunities and Timing ❏
c) Strength, Weight, Occupation and Threats ❏
d) Strengths, Weaknesses, Opportunities and Threats ❏

10. In the context of business, what does the acronym USP stand for?
a) Ultra Sensory Perception ❏
b) Ultimate Strategic Positioning ❏
c) Unique Selling Point ❏
d) Unique Selling Pitch ❏

Surviving in tough times

In an economic recession unemployment tends to go up and naturally there are fewer jobs available. In times like this it is necessary to take all the necessary steps to make sure that you go for the most suitable jobs for you as an individual, and use as many of the tools and techniques described in this book to be selected for interview and succeed in that interview.

Here are ten key tips to help you in difficult times:

1 Whatever your circumstances, direct your feelings and emotions towards problem-solving behaviour. All your emotional energy should go into finding the most suitable job. Avoid self-criticism and the criticism of previous employers.

2 Realize that your CV or resumé is a sales document. Its aim is to get you selected for interview. You are selling yourself, so what skills, abilities, experiences, personality traits, successes etc. are you selling and are these abilities what the prospective employer is looking for?

3 Be honest about yourself and carry out an individual SWOT analysis. What are your strengths with reference to the jobs you are going for and what are your weaknesses? Employers are looking for aptitude and interest in the role. You can be trained. Be aware of the external opportunities out there and also the threats.

4 Assume you will have to spend time on job search techniques. Be proactive, use networking, apply for jobs in companies you would like to work for but are not yet advertising. Scan newspapers, the internet, magazines etc. List all the avenues and use them. Physically tick them off as you go through them.

5 Acquaint yourself with new methods of promoting yourself and receiving information about jobs – the internet and social networking sites in particular.

6 Be careful, if not fastidious, about application forms, letters of application and your CV etc. Remember that first impressions count and employers are always looking for excuses to reduce the number of people they select for interview.

7 Do not expect instant success, especially in times of high unemployment. Remain motivated. Say to yourself, 'I have not failed to get an interview, the prospective employer has failed to appoint an enthusiastic, skilled employee!'

8 Always research the background of your prospective employer. The more you know about them, the more your CV will impress and the more you can impress the interviewers.

9 Remember your body language in the interview. You should come across as pleasant, alert and dynamic. It is not what you say – it is the way that you say it. Adopt the same mode of thinking as the interviewers.

10 If you end up with a large gap between jobs, consider self-employment. You may end up being permanently self-employed and successful. On the other hand, being self-employed shows initiative and drive and you might meet businesses that want you as part of their team.

Answers to questions

Sunday: 1c; 2b; 3a; 4d; 5d; 6c 7a;
8c; 9d; 10b.

Monday: 1d; 2b; 3c; 4c; 5b; 6a;
7d; 8d; 9d; 10c.

Tuesday: 1c; 2d; 3b; 4b; 5c; 6d;
7b; 8c; 9b; 10b.

Wednesday: 1d; 2d; 3c; 4b; 5a;
6c; 7a; 8d; 9b; 10a.

Thursday: 1b; 2a; 3d; 4c; 5d; 6a;
7b; 8d; 9a; 10c.

Friday: 1d; 2c; 3d; 4a; 5c; 6b; 7d;
8c; 9b; 10a.

Saturday: 1c; 2a; 3d; 4c; 5c; 6a;
7a; 8b; 9d; 10c.